VOLUME FOUR

ADVANCES IN TRANSPORT POLICY AND PLANNING

The Sharing Economy and The Relevance for Transport

VOLUME FOUR

ADVANCES IN TRANSPORT POLICY AND PLANNING

The Sharing Economy and The Relevance for Transport

Edited by

ELLIOT FISHMAN

Institute for Sensible Transport, Melbourne; Director of the Institute for Sensible Transport, Melbourne, VIC, Australia

ELSEVIER

ACADEMIC PRESS
An imprint of Elsevier

Academic Press is an imprint of Elsevier
50 Hampshire Street, 5th Floor, Cambridge, MA 02139, United States
525 B Street, Suite 1650, San Diego, CA 92101, United States
The Boulevard, Langford Lane, Kidlington, Oxford OX5 1GB, United Kingdom
125 London Wall, London, EC2Y 5AS, United Kingdom

First edition 2019

ISBN: 978-0-12-816210-1
ISSN: 2543-0009

For information on all Academic Press publications
visit our website at https://www.elsevier.com/books-and-journals

Publisher: Zoe Kruze
Acquisition Editor: Sam Mahfoudh
Editorial Project Manager: Shellie Bryant
Production Project Manager: James Selvam
Cover Designer: Alan Studholme

Typeset by SPi Global, India

Contents

Contributors

Vaughn Allan
Institute for Sensible Transport, Melbourne, Australia

Adam Cohen
McLaughlin Hall, University of California, Berkeley, CA, United States

Emily Farrar
McLaughlin Hall, University of California, Berkeley, CA, United States

Elliot Fishman
Institute for Sensible Transport, Melbourne; Director of the Institute for Sensible Transport, Melbourne, VIC, Australia

Cyriac George
The Institute of Transport Economics (TØI), Oslo, Norway

Krishna Murthy Gurumurthy
Department of Civil, Architectural and Environmental Engineering, The University of Texas at Austin, Austin, TX, United States

Tom Erik Julsrud
CICERO Center for International Climate Research, Oslo, Norway

Kara M. Kockelman
Department of Civil, Architectural and Environmental Engineering, The University of Texas at Austin, Austin, TX, United States

Benjamin J. Loeb
Delaware Valley Regional Planning Commission, Philadelphia, PA, United States

Susan Shaheen
McLaughlin Hall, University of California, Berkeley, CA, United States

Wijnand Veeneman
Delft University of Technology, Delft, The Netherlands

CHAPTER ONE

Introduction

Elliot Fishman*
Director of the Institute for Sensible Transport, Melbourne, VIC, Australia
*Corresponding author: e-mail address: info@sensibletransport.org.au

Abstract

This book details some of the current and future opportunities offered by the sharing economy within the transport and technology industry. It highlights that there has been rapid growth in the level of innovation from transport and technology companies, but for these advances to have maximum beneficial impact, government will need to provide stronger regulatory guidance, in the form of policies such as road user pricing.

Keywords: Mobility as a service, Driverless vehicle, Bike share, Road user pricing, Disruptive transport

The role of the Internet and mobile technology has acted as a platform for the sharing economy; everything from the sharing of houses, skills, office space and peer to peer lending is changing the face of commerce, and in fundamental ways, our society. At its best, the sharing economy is able to offer a better utilization of underused resources and even foster stronger communities by building personal relationships that may not have existed otherwise. While there are many facets of society that are being transformed by the sharing economy, arguably, nowhere is this more pronounced than the field of transport.

While the sharing of transport resources is not new (e.g., taxi services, borrowing friends/neighbors cars, and of course public transport), the ubiquity of the Internet has spawned a dramatic growth in the diversity of shared mobility options. This book offers a review of the literature on a wide range of shared mobility options, major technology trends and the implications of these developments for cities.

Why is the sharing economy of critical importance to transport? Transport presents one of the major challenges to enhancing the liveability, resilience and health of our cities. The growth in transport emissions, traffic congestion, noise and air pollution, as well as fatalities and serious injuries are just some of the major problems caused by the widespread use of the car that has occurred since the end of WWII. A well-recognized underlying

Advances in Transport Policy and Planning, Volume 4
ISSN 2543-0009
https://doi.org/10.1016/bs.atpp.2019.10.001

problem associated with car use and ownership is that while being one of the most expensive items people will buy in their lifetime, they sit idle for 95% of the day on average, making individual car ownership an example of very poor asset utilization. Moreover, each car is estimated to need between four and eight car parking bays in the city, driving up the cost of housing and limiting the space that can be used for more productive or useful purposes. The world's parking guru, Professor Donald Shoup has found that some 30% of downtown vehicle traffic is people circling for a car space. The average motor vehicle occupancy at peak hour is around 1.1 people per vehicle, despite the average car having five seats. As the world becomes increasingly urbanized and our cities denser, there is less space per person and this requires us to use space more efficiently. This book takes a look, through a variety of angles, at how the sharing economy can impact on the efficiency of our transport system.

Reversing the growth in transport emissions, lowering the rate of road death and serious injury, minimizing traffic congestion and enhancing the liveability of our cities has never been more important. To what extent can the sharing economy help address these issues? This volume takes a look at the literature on the sharing economy's impact on car use and other modes of transport. Given the fast pace of technological development, this chapter includes an analysis of the developments anticipated to be part of the transport system in coming years. Driverless cars, their impact on travel choice, car ownership and their place within the Mobility as a Service (MaaS) transformation is a critical topic within this chapter. What this book offers, is a review of the literature that considers both the potential benefits and unintended consequences that may arise from the transport sharing economy. Very often, especially within media articles on transport technology, the benefits of driverless vehicles (e.g., safety, lower private vehicle ownership) are discussed without consideration of the potential for downsides. For instance, talk of autonomous vehicles replacing traditional public transport might be possible for some outer suburban contexts, but the prospect of fleets of driverless cars carrying workers to dense central employment districts does not appear to acknowledge the space inefficiency of cars relative to public transport. A unifying theme within this chapter is the need to reduce unnecessary car use. The rationale for this is succinctly captured in Fig. 1. The black balloons represent emissions and the foot print represents space consumption. As the sharing economy continues to disrupt the transport sector and our cities, it will become increasingly important to frame the policy debate and regulatory conditions with the issue of *space* and *emissions*

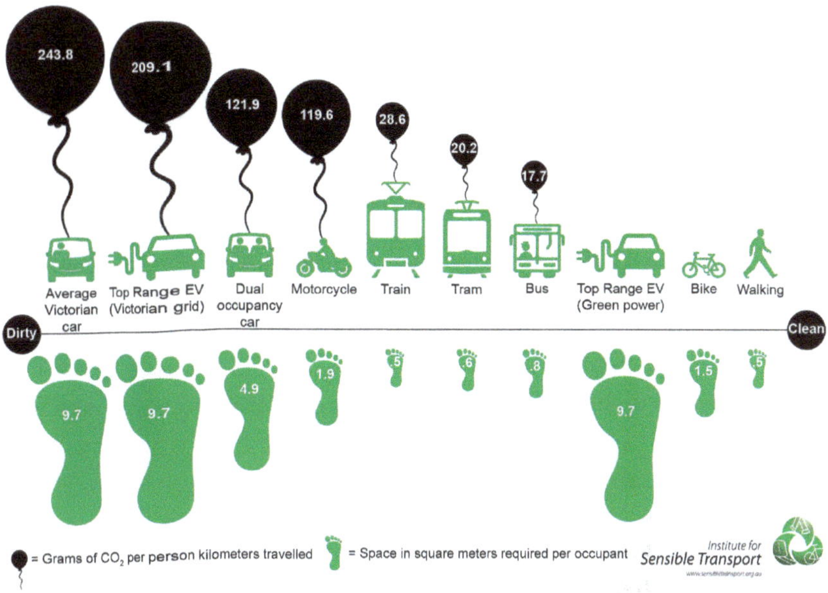

Fig. 1 Emissions and space consumption of various modes. NB: these have been calculated based on the occupancy rates and emissions intensity of Melbourne, Australia and are likely to vary slightly depending on the different energy mix and public transport occupancy in different cities.

in mind. A good example of where the absence of these conditions can exacerbate transport problems can be seen from cities such as New York, where the role of prominent sharing economy services such as Uber and Lyft have in fact been found to *increase* congestion.

This is also an important opportunity to distinguish between what is sharing, and what is simply the use of a tech platform to run a taxi service. Uber, Lyft and similar services are better described as e-hailing or ride sourcing services. These ride sourcing services should not strictly be considered part of the sharing economy, as the driver is only making the trip to take passengers. This is distinct from other services, such as BlaBlaCar, which match a driver intending to take a trip with a passenger with a compatible journey.

As driverless, shared mobility becomes closer to reality as an everyday mode of transport, there has never been a better time for a mature debate about the role of cars in cities. It is an opportunity to "re-set the clock" and take a fresh approach on the optimal mix of transport modes in cities. Much of the transport literature points to an overuse of motor vehicles, bringing with it all the problems identified above. And while driverless cars are often mentioned in the same breath of the sharing economy, it is entirely possible that, at least in the first few decades of their introduction, they are owned in the same manner as conventional cars are now. Should this occur, it is more than plausible that these cars may cause an *increase* in driving. The mechanisms through which this might occur are complex, but may involve:

1. People who are too young or old to drive will be able to summon a ride. Some of these people may have been chauffeured previously, but some will be either making a trip they would not otherwise have made, or do so by autonomous vehicle rather than use another mode (e.g., public transport, bicycle).
2. Pooled autonomous vehicles may be able to compete on price with public transport. Even if the cost is slightly higher than public transport, many trips may be substantially quicker than the same trip by public transport and this may result in a drop in public transport use.
3. By not having to focus on driving, the rider avoids the "time cost" driving, which may increase their willingness to travel further or spend more time in congested traffic.
4. Cars may be able to drive without any occupants. While this may reduce demand for car parking, it is likely to exacerbate congestion by increasing vehicle kilometers traveled (VKT).

For the reasons identified above, it is of critical importance that the potential impacts of emerging technologies be considered carefully rather than blindly adopted without consideration for their potential impacts.

In "Cars and the sharing economy: The emergence and impacts of shared automobility in the urban environment," Cyriac George and Tom Julsrud review the literature on new ways in which technology is allowing for the sharing of cars. Their review also looks at the degree to which these services impact on overall automobile use. This chapter identifies that existing regulatory frameworks are not well equipped to handle the competition expected between incumbents and new entrants.

Public transport is often overlooked, or even seen as being redundant when looking at the emerging transport technology that is purported to be at the heart of the MaaS eco-system. In "Public transport in a sharing environment," Wijnand Veeneman examines the role these disruptive transport technologies may play, either as complementary or competitive forces within the existing public transport system. He finds that the degree to which these new offerings are able to support the sustainability of the transport system is very much dependent on the role government plays in regulating these services. If left entirely to the market, there is the potential for future services like "robo-taxis" to exacerbate congestion problems. At its best shared mobility could help make up for the weaknesses in public transport, proving to be an effective first/last mile solution to public transport.

In "Sharing vehicles and sharing rides in real time: Opportunities for self driving fleets," Gurumurthy et al. explore the emergence of shared and fully automated vehicles, especially in terms of impacts these developments might have for the creation of fleets of MaaS driverless vehicles. They find that each shared, driverless vehicle can replace six or more privately owned vehicles in wealthy countries where car ownership is high. One of the potentially problematic outcomes of widespread fleets of driverless cars is zero-occupancy vehicles. The authors found that regional government regulation will be required to ensure these future fleets of autonomous vehicles do not exacerbate the impact of cars in our cities.

Car share is one of the most established forms of transport within the sharing economy. Susan Shaheen et al. in "Car sharing's impact and future" describes the current car share market, the different types of car share available and some of the changes expected to impact on car share from vehicle technology and MaaS platforms. This chapter also reviews the literature regarding the impacts of existing car share services, and offers insights into how developments such as electric and autonomous vehicles might change the very nature of how people access cars in the future. Importantly, Shaheen et al. find that road user pricing fees may be necessary to manage the demand for road space and this again touches on a unifying theme with the book: technologies cannot be introduced without consideration for how the regulatory environment will need to adapt to account for the pressures the sharing economy may place on an already strained transport system.

Shared transport is not solely focused on four wheeled vehicles of course, and the burgeoning two wheeled shared transport sector has been especially active and innovative over the last 5 years. The number of shared use bicycles has ballooned to over 4.5 million, and many of these bikes are dockless systems that rely on GPS and other technologies to track bikes and integrate with smartphones to unlock and pay for the bikes. Given that so many of the trips in our increasingly urbanized world are short (less than 5 km), shared bicycles are well placed to provide space efficient mobility that is also healthy, pollution free and does not exert the level of road traffic danger on other road users in the same way motor vehicles do. In "Bike share," Elliot Fishman and Vaughn Allan review the literature on a range of bike

competition with incumbent modes, safety regulations and labor conditions. We have begun to see signs of consolidation among ride-sharing and ride-sourcing. Further technological innovations may lead to further consolidations with car sharing.

Keywords: Sharing economy, Car sharing, Shared automobility, Urban development

1. Introduction

This chapter examines innovative forms of urban automobile transport that are part of the emerging "sharing economy." We will refer to these using the umbrella term "shared automobility." As with the broader sharing economy, shared automobility is characterized by a shift from ownership of material assets to temporary access. Whereas scholars and policymakers generally agree that the implications of this shift will be profound and far reaching, there is more disagreement as to whether these changes will be good for society. Such discussions typically focus on local environmental impacts, climate emissions, traffic congestion, public safety, transportation modality, and labor rights.

This chapter highlights themes and findings from a selection of 53 scholarly articles and other publications related to ride-sharing, ride-sourcing and car sharing. Based on this, we point out gaps in the literature and recommend paths for future research.[a] We work toward conceptual clarity by emphasizing the importance of shared automobility as an umbrella term and the relationship between the modes therein. The value of this is crucial given that most forms of shared automobility are relatively new; that they have undergone significant changes since their respective inceptions; and that it is highly unlikely that they will remain as they are today in the coming years, especially in light of emerging technologies like autonomous driving.

The three types of shared automobility covered in this chapter are car sharing, ride-sharing, and ride-sourcing. Car sharing refers to "a practice whereby registered members of an organization or platform can rent and operate vehicles on a self-access basis for short- and medium-term use" (George and Julsrud, 2018). Ride-sharing refers to the "adding (of) additional passengers to a pre-existing trip" (SUMC, 2015); this includes traditional or informal carpooling as well as real-time dynamic ride-sharing

[a] This chapter is not intended to be a systematic literature review—there exist already good reviews that cover different aspects of shared automobility (Agatz et al., 2012; Ferguson, 1997; Jittrapirom et al., 2017; Jorge and Correia, 2013).

through apps. Ride-sourcing, or ride-hailing, refers to digital platforms that connect passengers with the owners of private vehicle who are willing to drive them to a destination for a fee; the most prominent of such platforms are Uber and Lyft.

We seek, furthermore, to highlight the important strands of discourse concerning cars and sharing, especially as they relate to urban areas. Insofar as sustainability is a recurrent theme in the literature on mobility and the sharing economy, this chapter addresses sustainable mobility in the urban environment and gives less attention to the ways in which sustainable mobility modes are taken up at the user or household level(s).

The literature selected for review in this chapter was compiled using Google Scholar, and ScienceDirect databases using the key words: ride-sharing, ride-sourcing, car sharing, shared mobility, sharing economy, carpooling, transportation network companies and shared automobility. The chapter will be organized into the following sections: The sharing economy and its cousins (Section 2), Automobility, shared mobility and shared automobility (Section 3), Key research findings and impacts of shared automobility (Section 4), and Conclusion, synthesis and challenges looking ahead (Section 5).

2. The sharing economy and its cousins

The "sharing economy" is a term used to describe recent changes in the way individual economic agents consume resources and services. This is not to suggest, however, that sharing itself is new. Sharing predates not only modern transportation technology, but humanity itself. The propensity to share resources and cooperate were fundamental attributes that we inherited from our primate ancestors—without them we never would have survived as a species (Fukuyama, 2011; Price, 1975). The conceptualization that emphasizes the human as being a self-interested individual (consumer) is a more modern development. Simply put, sharing has always existed. What, however, are the recent changes that seemingly justify the use of the term sharing economy?

The Oxford English Dictionary defines the verb "share" as to "Give a portion of (something) to another or others" or "Use, occupy, or enjoy (something) jointly with another or others" (OED, 2019). The emphasis here should be on the word "others." Until recently, sharing, as opposed to purely economic transactions, was limited to ones trusted social network, which was largely comprised of family, friends and neighbors. Recent advances in information and communication technology (ICT), particularly as they relate to smartphones and broadband connectivity have enabled sharing among a much broader set of agents, most notably strangers—"digital platforms are able to make stranger sharing less risky and more appealing because they source information on users via the use of ratings and reputations" (Frenken and Schor, 2017; Schor, 2016).

The form of interactions and exchange taking place within the sharing economy is narrower and more transaction oriented than general social sharing that is common within families or between friends. The distinction resembles to some extent the concepts of "sharing in" and "sharing out." While sharing in is the common consumption of resources within a denser circle of people who often regard property as being common, sharing out involves consuming with others outside the social group's boundaries (Ingold, 1986). Sharing out is therefor closer to gift giving and economic transactions (Belk, 2010).

Lawrence Lessig, who is often cited as the first person to use the term "sharing economy." also recognized that while sharing has always existed, the fundamental change occurred when ICT enabled us to formalize and monetize that which had previously been informal and voluntary (Lessig, 2008). He describes this as a shift from "thick" to "thin" sharing. Thick sharing refers to sharing in which there is a mutual benefit for all the parties engaged in the transaction, i.e., it is not a purely self-interested act. Such behavior is consistent with the sharing exhibited by member of a trusted or tightknit community. Thin sharing on the other hand is more focused on individual gain and resembles the self-interested actor model within classical economics. In recent years, there has been an increase in the amount of thin sharing in the world. Lessig explains that "a thin sharing economy is often easier to support than a think sharing economy …(because)…all things being equal, a me motivation (for us, now) comes more easily to most" (Lessig, 2008, p. 155). Lessig defines the sharing economy as "collaborative consumption made by the activities of sharing, exchanging, and rental of resources without owning the goods." (Lessig, 2008, p. 143). Although this definition captures the broad shift from ownership to access, it includes several types of consumption that are worth considering on their own and in relation to one another.

This chapter adopts a more recent definition of the sharing economy: "consumers granting each other temporary access to under-utilized physical assets (idle capacity), possibly for money" (Frenken et al., 2015; Frenken and Schor, 2017).[b] There are three constituent elements to this definition that

[b] For a more detailed description of the various definitions of sharing economy and contestations thereof, see Puschmann and Alt (2016) and Gruszka (2017).

are worth addressing separately: (1) consumer-to-consumer (C2C), or peer-to-peer (P2P) relationships; (2) temporary access; and (3) physical asset. Off the bat, this comes into conflict with many popular contemporary descriptions of the sharing economy.

In order to resolve these conflicting accounts and get the most out of this definition, it is worthwhile to situate the sharing economy in relation to these "close cousins." Although these close cousins distinguish themselves with respect to the strict definition of the sharing economy, the former remain relevant because they are strongly associated with the changes characterized by the latter. As such, this chapter discusses the shared use of automobiles in light of the sharing economy as well as its close cousins.

Firstly, the C2C nature of the sharing economy excludes business to consumer transactions. The relevance of this cannot be overlooked considering the desire among companies to portray themselves as being part of the sharing economy because it is perceived to be "trendy" (Gruszka, 2017). This is not to suggest that these companies' claims are completely without merit—many are part of the related *product-service economy*. Daimler's subsidiary car sharing company Car2go, and BMW's own DriveNow, which recently merged to form the joint venture, Share Now, offers consumers temporary access to physical assets and are examples are prominent platforms in the product-service economy.

Most studies of product-service economies have focused on the economic perspective of the firms that provide the services. In a literature review of product-service economies, Beuren et al. (2013) claim that more attention must be given in future research to its environmental and social impacts. In particular, there needs to be a better understanding of the cultural changes associated with the consumer transition from ownership to services.

Secondly, temporary access implies that the provider in the transaction maintains ownership of the item in question. This excludes recycling or the resale or giving away of goods, which are, nevertheless, in the related category known as the *second-hand economy*. eBay, which facilitates the buying and selling of physical assets on a C2C basis, would be an example of a prominent platform in the second-hand economy (although not exclusively, given that the company also facilitates the sale of new goods). This also delimits the sharing economy from general definitions of sharing in social communities, that describe sharing as granting free access to collective resources without any time limits (Belk, 2010). As this conception of the sharing economy come closer to lending than traditional sharing, which can be seen as a borderline case of sharing (Tinson and Nutall, 2008).

Thirdly, the sharing economy is fundamentally about physical assets. This excludes transactions that involve the provision of a service, even though said provision requires the use of a physical asset. Uber and Lyft, which facilitate C2C transaction that involve temporary access, are examples of prominent platforms in the *on-demand, or "gig" economy*. This chapter examines new forms of automobile use that encompasses the sharing economy, as well as the related product-service, second-hand, and on-demand economies.

It is important to consider the product-service economy, the second-hand economy and the on-demand economy in conjunction with the broader sharing economy for two reasons: (1) the popular discourse of the sharing economy includes these close cousins and given that they are driven by similar technological and social changes, they are relevant to one another; and (2) it should not be taken for granted that the boundaries between these economies will remain static—further technological and social change may transform our mobility systems in ways that demand more comprehensive and adaptable conceptual frameworks if we are to make sense of them.

3. Automobility, shared mobility and shared automobility

Automobile use has benefits as well as costs. There is increased recognition among researchers and policy makers that the social, economic and environmental costs of automobility is too high, especially in urban areas (Becker et al., 2012; Geels et al., 2011; Walks, 2014). Automobility here refers not merely to the use of a vehicle to travel from one place to another, but the systemic manner in which the private consumption of a manufactured object (i.e., the automobile) provides social meaning to consumers and transforms the society and environment that facilitates the consumption, while at the same time subordinating all other competing modes of mobility (Urry, 2004). This is to say that any change to the current dominant model or urban mobility would not only have profound implications, but would require adjustments of deeply entrenched technologies, institutions and practices.

Importantly, there has been a shift in thinking from the speed-promoting mentality of automobility, which sought to provide favorable regulations and exclusive real estate for private vehicular movement and parking, toward an efficiency and sustainability oriented mentality that assumes that there is an acceptable or optimal level of congestion that urban areas should have (Banister, 2008). A requisite assumption in such a shift involves shared modes of mobility. The simplest way to conceptualize shared mobility is to posit it against private mobility. Although private mobility can be as simple as walking or bicycling, it is in contrast to the private use of automobiles in urban areas that shared mobility is most often described. Lately, the sustainable mobility paradigm has been overshadowed by the concept of smart mobility, where automobility has been given a role as an integrated element in an urban environment that is coordinated and controlled by digital networks (Albino et al., 2015; Lyons, 2018). In this vision the car has lost its status as a privately-owned resource, to the benefit of a seamless web of transport services across various modes.

The Shared-Use Mobility Center (SUMC) identifies the following as examples of shared mobility: bike sharing, car sharing, ride-sourcing, ride-sharing, public transit, e-bike and scooter sharing, micro-transit, shuttles, taxis & limousines, jitneys, aggregators, flexible commercial delivery, mobility huts (SUMC, 2015). Of these, there are four that focus exclusively on automobile use—car sharing, ride-sourcing, ride-sharing, taxi/limousine.

Ride-sharing encompasses traditional carpooling and real-time dynamic ride-sharing, both of which involve coupling passengers in need of a ride with pre-existing trips. Although the former generally refers to informal arrangements that have existed since the beginning of the automobile age, the ICT trends typical of the broader sharing economy have brought about services like SoMo (short for social mobility), which is an app that allows users in the Washington, DC area to plan and organize recurring trips to common destinations among friends, family members and co-workers. Most ride-sharing efforts have focused on commuters as the main "user." High-occupancy vehicle (HOV) lanes are a common and time-tested approach. Nevertheless, in countries like the United States, carpooling has been in steady decline since its peak in the 1970s (Ferguson, 1997) despite the arrival of promising new technological opportunities (Shaheen et al., 2018). Of the forms of shared automobility covered in this chapter, ride-sharing is the one that falls closest within the strict definition of sharing economy.

Ride-sourcing often attracts the most attention in discussions on the sharing economy, in large part because it is the one that comes in most direct conflict with incumbent mobility providers, namely taxis. Ride-sourcing platforms connect passengers via smartphone to private vehicle owners who accept a fee for the trip. Ride-sourcing platforms, the most prominent ones of which are Uber and Lyft, are often also referred to as transportation network companies (TNCs). Such terminology allows the TNC to avoid many of the regulatory responsibilities of a traditional transportation service provider, while simultaneously allowing local authorities to incorporate these new companies into the regulatory framework of the broader urban mobility system. In recent years, TNCs have experimented with allowing multiple passengers with similar destinations to share a hired vehicle—a practice known as dynamic ride-sharing, which serves as a form of decentralized micro-transit.

Whereas ride-sourcing has existed for approximately a decade, and car-pooling has largely been an informal practice until recently, formal *car sharing* has been around for decades. Car sharing is "a practice whereby registered members of an organization or platform can rent and operate vehicles on a self-access basis for short- and medium-term use" (George and Julsrud, 2018). The earliest attempt at establishing a formal car sharing organization stretch back to the late 1940s in Switzerland; the following decades saw similar attempts in other European cities (Millard-Ball, 2005; Shaheen and Cohen, 2007). Most of these early attempts failed as a result of technological and organizational limitations—it was not until the 1980s, in Switzerland and Germany, that the first viable car sharing organizations emerged (Harms and Truffer, 1998). Car sharing platforms are often differentiated from one another based on business model and operational model. The main business models for car sharing include business-to-consumer (B2C), which is the most traditional, business-to-business (B2B), and most recently, peer-to-peer (P2P). The main operational models for car sharing platforms are (1) station based (or round trip), whereby users must pick up and return the vehicle to the same place, (2) free-floating (or one-way) whereby users can drop off a vehicle at any legal parking spot within a predetermined geographic area, and (3) P2P whereby users and providers make private arrangements for pick-up and delivery. The P2P segment, which spans business and organizational models, would be the only type of car sharing that would fall under the strict definition of sharing economy. The other types are all part of the related product-service economy.

4. Literature and key findings of shared automobility

We reviewed a total of 53 articles that focus on the three main types of shared automobility described in the previous section. Each type of shared mobility is linked with one or more of the themes that are used to judge their impact on the urban mobility system and society at large. These themes include environmental impact, congestion, vehicle holdings, VKT, market/regulation, and public health.

The literature on ride-sharing is some of the first scholarly works on the impacts of shared mobility, but this refers to informal carpooling arrangements. Ferguson (1997) was mostly concerned with explaining why carpooling in the United States had declined so much since its peak in the 1970s; important factors included the reduction in automobile and fuel costs as well as increased education among the general population.

In the last couple of years, more attention has been given to dynamic ride-sharing platforms. More often than not, however, this is considered to be an extension of ride-sourcing rather than a maturation of carpooling. In almost all instances, ride-sharing is associated with positive environmental impacts, although the benefits were more pronounced in urban and dense areas (Albinsson and Perera, 2018; Javid et al., 2016, 2017). The effects on public transit, however, are mixed. In some cases, carpoolers were more likely to be commuters that previously took public transit (Shaheen et al., 2016). In others, car sharing was seen as an effective feeder for multi-modal mobility (Agatz et al., 2012). Martinez and Viegas (2017) consider ride-sharing in an autonomous vehicle future and emphasize that environmental and congestion benefits accrue only if walkable and transit oriented land use is maintained and the overall number of vehicles decline as a result of sharing. According to Fagnant and Kockelman's (2018) simulation, although shared autonomous vehicles can "lower household vehicle ownership rates, lower parking requirements, traveler cost savings, and significant operator profit opportunities," overall reductions in VKT are only going to be achieved if dynamic ride-sharing is promoted so as to avoid empty driving during relocation.

The literature on ride-sourcing is more developed and covers a wide range of themes, the most prominent of which are impacts on congestion and the environment, public health and the need for new market and regulatory frameworks.

The effects of ride-sourcing on congestion are complex and dependent on context. Li et al. (2016b) found that the introduction of Uber into a market was associated with significant reductions in congestion, with the potential causal mechanisms being reduced car ownership among users, increase in dynamic ride-sharing and avoidance of travel during peak hours. Hall et al. (2018) found that although ride-sourcing provided a good feeder for public transit, especially in cities with underdeveloped public transit infrastructure, it still resulted in longer commutes and may be a contributing factor to increased congestion. Such effects may also depend on the number of operators present in a city—Sadowsky and Nelson (2017) found that the presence of one ride-sourcing provider in a market complemented the public transit system, whereas the presence of two operators unleashed competitive forces that resulted in increased substitution of public transit. Mishra and Clewlow (2017) have found that ride-sourcing competes mostly with inner urban public transit but that it complements commuter rail services, which typically cover longer distances and suburban areas. Despite the potential conflict between ride-sourcing and public transit, the latter is still seen as an indispensable part of any future urban mobility system (Basu et al., 2018).

The disruptions brought about by ride-sourcing places pressure on the regulatory frameworks that are currently outdated and unprepared to deal with such changes. Shared automobility will inevitably come into conflict with certain incumbent modes, but they will not go away; we need experimental regulations that find a way to incorporates shared automobility modes into the overall mobility system (Posen, 2015). Further disruptions are to be expected. If and when sourced vehicles are operated autonomously, the taxi industry will be hit hardest and new regulations would be needed to ensure that this disruption to the urban mobility system takes place in a manner that is fair and effective (Aarhaug and Olsen, 2018).

Unlike with the other two forms of shared automobility, a significant amount of the research literature on ride-sourcing focuses on public health issues, especially the prevalence of automobile collisions as a result of driving under the influence of alcohol or other narcotics. There are several studies that provide evidence that ride-sourcing leads to reductions in vehicle collision (Greenwood and Wattal, 2017; Martin-Buck, 2017; Morrison et al., 2017). Peck (2017) adds that such benefits are limited to densely populated areas. This runs somewhat in contrast with Martin-Buck (2017) who found that areas with less developed public transit—typically outside of the urban core—experienced the strongest reductions in alcohol-related collisions. In some instances, Uber presence was associated with reductions not only in collisions but also arrests for assault and disorderly conduct, which may be related to alcohol consumption (Dills and Mulholland, 2018).

Most of the research on car sharing looks at its environmental impact as measured by vehicle holdings and VKT. In general, car sharing users own fewer cars and drive less. Car sharing can lead to reduced vehicle holdings when members sell a car they already own, delay the purchase of a car, or forgo the purchase of a car. Car sharing generally attracts users who do not already own a vehicle. Sioui et al. (2013) found that only 12% of Montreal car sharing users owned a car as compared with 66% for the general population. In one of the earlier studies on the impacts of car sharing, Katzev (1999) found that 26% of members in Carsharing Portland sold a vehicle within the first year of membership with an additional 53% who delayed such a purchase. Although most users planned to or did buy a car eventually, as long as they are replaced by new members who also delay or avoid purchasing, the effect on vehicle holdings is still a net reduction. Cervero and Tsai (2004) found that members of San Francisco's CityShare were twice as likely to sell a car or delay the purchase of one as compared with non-members. In a follow-up study (Cervero et al., 2007), members were 12% more likely to shed a vehicle. Firnkorn and Müller (2011) found that 13.5% of car2go members expected to reduce their vehicle holdings as a result of car sharing. Even among newer forms of car sharing like free-floating or one-way platforms, users are more likely to reduce their car ownership (Becker et al., 2017).

At the corporate level car sharing has been shown to offer an alternative to maintaining company fleets. Shaheen and Stocker (2015) found approximately 20% of corporate members of Zipcar sold a vehicle as a result of membership while an additional 20% postponed purchase, which corresponds to a total reduction of approximately 33,000 vehicles.

Although the results are not consistent in all contexts, car sharing members generally drive less than non-members (Cervero et al., 2007; Loose, 2010; Martin and Shaheen, 2011; Nijland and van Meerkerk, 2017; Steininger et al., 1996). A popular criticism of car sharing, however, is that it leads to more driving among people who would have otherwise driven less—a phenomenon that can be described as having to do with "induced demand" (Cervero, 2003; Walb and Loudon, 1986). While it is true that going from no access to a car to having access to a car will almost always lead to more driving, we must consider the alternatives. In other words, the increase in driving as a result of using car sharing must be compared alongside the increase that would have taken place if these users had purchased a car. Steininger et al. (1996) found that among car sharing users in Austria, households that did not previously own a car saw a VKT increase in 118% whereas households that did own a car beforehand saw a decrease of 62%. Still, the first group started out from a much lower baseline—"In absolute per person terms the increase of the latter group is only one sixth the reduction of the former group. The aggregate net effect...was a reduction of 53%." Lane (2005) found similar results in Philadelphia where households that did not have a car beforehand saw a VKT increase of 48 km/month whereas households that did have a car beforehand saw a decrease of approximately 840 km/month. In short, the many instances of induced demand are weighed out by the fewer but more dramatic decreases in demand.

The following table compiles 53 articles on ride-sharing, ride-sourcing and car sharing and some related practices associated with the sharing economy and shared automobility (Table 1).

5. Synthesis and discussion and challenges looking ahead

The practices associated with the sharing economy are a relatively new phenomena, despite the continuous presence of sharing across human history. Just as sharing has always been around, people have shared cars for as long as they have existed. In the early days of the automobile age this was largely because of cars were prohibitively expensive. There have also been trigger events like the world wars and the oil crisis of the 1970s that encouraged sharing of cars—it was during the latter, for example, that carpooling peaked in the United States. The emergence of the sharing economy and the ubiquity of the Internet over the last couple of decades that has opened up new ways of sharing automobiles.

The most notable of these are ride-sharing, ride-sourcing, and car sharing, which will be categorize collectively as shared automobility. Shared automobility provides an umbrella term to capture the modes of mobility that fall under the rubric of the sharing economy and its close cousins.

5.1 Regulation and market

A consistent theme across the literature is that the new forms of mobility enabled by the sharing economy run into conflict with the established practices and regulatory frameworks of incumbent urban mobility systems. Whether this relates to competition with taxis, fair labor conditions or safety standards, shared automobility as a whole is not going away. Most of the urban mobility regulatory frameworks were designed for the private automobile as the dominant mode—the challenges associated with shared automobility require new regulations that accommodates the new technologies and practices that are being adopted rapidly across the globe.

Government regulations, from the national to the municipal levels, are outdated and authorities are either scared or unprepared to adapt to changing

Table 1 Literature on shared automobility.

Article	Title	Type of sharing	Theme/criteria	General findings, notes
Briceno et al. (2005)	Using life cycle approaches to evaluate sustainable consumption programs: car sharing	Car sharing	Env. Broad	If money saved from car sharing is used on a distributed set of consumables, the carbon impact is marginal, but if spent on, e.g., air travel, carbon reductions diminish
Doka and Ziegler (2001)	Complete life cycle assessment for vehicle models of the mobility carsharing fleet Switzerland	Car sharing	Env. Broad	As cars become more efficient, the share of carbon footprint derived from land use and material consumption increases
Hertwich (2005)	Consumption and the rebound effect: An industrial ecology perspective	Car sharing	Env. Broad	Rebound effect: changed behavior may offset part of the environmental gain
Chen and Kockelman (2016)	Carsharing's life cycle impacts on energy use and greenhouse gas emissions	Car sharing	Env. Broad	Individual reduction in energy use and GHG emission by 51% and net savings expected to be 3% across all US households
Cervero et al. (2007)	City CarShare: longer-term travel demand and car ownership impacts	Car sharing	Vehicle hold VKT	Members were 12% more likely to shed a vehicle than non-members. VKT decrease of 67% for members, 24% increase for non-members
E. Martin et al. (2010)	Impact of carsharing on household vehicle holdings: Results from North American shared-use vehicle survey	Car sharing	Vehicle hold	carsharing removed between 9 and 13 vehicles from the road for each shared vehicle deployed
Firnkorn and Müller (2011)	What will be the environmental effects of new free-floating car-sharing systems? The case of car2go in Ulm	Car sharing	Vehicle hold	Expected reduction in vehicle holdings by 13.5% among members and an overall reduction in CO_2 emissions by 53–60%

Continued

Table 1 Literature on shared automobility.—Cont'd

Article	Title	Type of sharing	Theme/criteria	General findings, notes
Becker et al. (2012)	Comparing car-sharing schemes in Switzerland: User groups and usage patterns	Car sharing	Vehicle hold	6% of free-floating car sharing customers reduced their car ownership, as compared to a group of non-users
Katzev (1999)	Carsharing Portland: Review and analysis of its first year	Car sharing	Vehicle hold	Nearly 80% of members either sold a vehicle or postponed the purchase of one
Nijland and van Meerkerk (2017)	Mobility and environmental impacts of car sharing in the Netherlands	Car sharing	Vehicle hold VKT	Members reduced vehicle holdings by 30% and drove 15–20% less as compared with
S Shaheen and Stocker (2015)	Carsharing for Business, Zipcar Case Study & Impact Analysis	Car sharing	Vehicle hold	1 in 5 corporate members sold a vehicle and 1 in 5 postponed the purchase of vehicle due to joining Zipcar—total reduction of approx. 33,000 vehicles
Sioui et al. (2013)	How carsharing affects the travel behavior of households: a case study of Montréal, Canada	Car sharing	Vehicle hold	Members much less likely to own a car
Walb and Loudon (1986)	Evaluation of the Short-Term Auto Rental (STAR) Service in San Francisco, CA	Car sharing	Vehicle hold VKT	Overall driving among members went up but many ceased ownership of a private vehicle following start of membership
Baptista et al. (2014)	Energy, environmental and mobility impacts of car-sharing systems. Empirical results from Lisbon, Portugal	Car sharing	VKT	Well to wheel (WTW) emission reduction of hybrid electric vehicles and 35% in hybrid cars and 65% in BEVs

Cervero and Tsai (2004)	City CarShare in San Francisco, California: second-year travel demand and car ownership impacts	Car sharing	VKT	Mean VMT fell by 47% for members and increased by nearly 73% for non-members. In absolute terms, the emissions reductions among members were much larger than the increase among non-members
Cervero (2003)	City CarShare: First-year travel demand impacts	Car sharing	VKT	Members' net VMT was 19.5–54.3% higher than non-members
Martin and Shaheen (2011)	Greenhouse gas emission impacts of carsharing in North America	Car sharing	VKT	Members saw a 27–43% reduction in VMT and a corresponding 34–41% reduction in GHG emissions
Lane (2005)	PhillyCarShare: First-year social and mobility impacts of carsharing in Philadelphia, Pennsylvania	Car sharing	VKT	Users who gained access to a car increased their VMT by up to 48 km/month whereas members who gave up ownership of a car reduced their VMT by up to 840 km/month. Each shared car replaced 23 private vehicles
Loose (2010)	The state of European car sharing	Car sharing	VKT	An overall reduction in CO_2 emissions by 15–20%
Steininger et al. (1996)	Car-sharing organizations: The size of the market segment and revealed change in mobility behavior	Car sharing	VKT	Members who did not previously own a car saw an increased VKT of 118% whereas those who previously owned saw a decrease in 62%. However, in absolute terms, the reductions were much larger

Continued

Table 1 Literature on shared automobility.—Cont'd

Article	Title	Type of sharing	Theme/criteria	General findings, notes
Cohen and Kietzmann (2014)	Ride On! Mobility Business Models for the Sharing Economy	General	Market	Complete privatization of transit would fail to optimize service or environmental impact. Merit based business models would aid in public-private partnerships
Davidson and Infranca (2016)	The Sharing Economy as an Urban Phenomenon	General	Market	Previous tech disruptions involved national regulations; shared mobility is more municipal and geographically distributed. Need new and holistic local regulations
Martin (2016)	The sharing economy: A pathway to sustainability or a nightmarish form of neoliberal capitalism?	General	Review	Although the sharing economy was rooted in sustainable consumption and economic opportunity, corporate cooptation will make these goals less likely
Malhotra and Van Alstyne (2014)	The Dark Side of the Sharing Economy … and How to Lighten It	General	Review	New market and regulatory framework is needed to ensure against unfair competition, labor without dignity, discrimination and public safety risks
Reim et al. (2015)	Product-Service Systems (PSS) business models and tactics–a systematic literature review	General	Review	Three types of business models (product-, use,- and result-oriented) are linked with operational tactics for implementation success and value generation: contracts, marketing, networks, product/service design and sustainability

Meijkamp (1998)	Changing consumer behavior through eco-efficient services: an empirical study of car sharing in the Netherlands	General	VKT	Members saw a 33% reduction in total driving
Jittrapirom et al. (2017)	Mobility as a service: A critical review of definitions, assessments of schemes, and key challenges	MaaS	Review	MaaS provides a conceptual framework that integrates multiple forms of shared mobility, automobile-based and not, in a single platform
Ou and Tang (2018)	Impacts of carpooling on trip costs under car-following model	Ride-sharing	Congestion	Carpooling can relieve traffic congestion
Javid et al. (2017)	Quantifying the environmental impacts of increasing high occupancy vehicle lanes in the United States	Ride-sharing	EnvironmentCongestion	Expanding HOV lanes better at encouraging carpooling in more populous and urban areas with greatest emissions reductions in densely populated areas
Javid et al. (2016)	The environmental impacts of carpooling in the United States	Ride-sharing	Environment	Carpooling by means of HOV lanes are effective at reducing emissions, but mostly in urban areas
Minett and Pearce (2011)	Estimating the energy consumption impact of casual carpooling	Ride-sharing	Environment	Casual carpooling reduces energy use
Susan Shaheen and Cohen (2018)	Shared ride services in North America: definitions, impacts, and the future of pooling	Ride-sharing	Environment Congestion Cost	Carpooling will merge with autonomous vehicles with benefits accruing only with enough sharing
Ferguson (1997)	The rise and fall of the American carpool: 1970–90	Ride-sharing	Review	Increased vehicle availability, low fuel costs and higher education among drivers led to reduced carpooling. Other smaller factors include: age, sex, racial diversity, urban form and relative poverty

Continued

Table 1 Literature on shared automobility.—Cont'd

Article	Title	Type of sharing	Theme/criteria	General findings, notes
S. A. Shaheen et al. (2016)	Casual carpooling in the San Francisco Bay Area: Understanding user characteristics, behaviors, and motivations	Ride-sharing	Users Modality	Convenience and saved time and money were important motivations. Community and environment less important. Most carpoolers were former public transit riders
Albinsson and Perera (2018)	Assessing the impact of real-time ride-sharing on urban traffic using mobile phone data	Ride-sharing (dynamic)	Congestion	Can reduce congestion (both VMT and VHT) but only if adopters are former car drivers. More effective for urban areas and shorter trips
Fagnant and Kockelman (2018)	Dynamic ride-sharing and fleet sizing for a system of shared autonomous vehicles in Austin, Texas	Ride-sharing (dynamic)	Congestion VKT Automation	Shared autonomous fleets can reduce vehicle holdings, parking requirements and cost, but reductions in VKT are only possible with effective dynamic ride-sharing systems
Martinez and Viegas (2017)	Assessing the impacts of deploying a shared self-driving urban mobility system: An agent-based model applied to the city of Lisbon, Portugal	Ride-sharing (dynamic)	Environment Congestion	Model suggests that maintaining metro service and replacing private car, bus and taxi mobility with shared autonomous modes would significantly reduce and CO_2 emissions and congestion
Agatz et al. (2012)	Optimization for dynamic ride-sharing: A review	Ride-sharing (dynamic)	Review	Technical (algorithmic) barriers remain for optimal performance. Ride-sharing can serve as a feeder for multi-modal transit

Li et al. (2016a)	An empirical analysis of on-demand ride-sharing and traffic congestion	Ride-sourcing	Congestion	Uber entry was associated with significant reductions in congestion with potential mechanisms being reduced car ownership, increase in ride-sharing and avoidance of travel during peak hours
Feng et al. (2017)	We are on the way: Analysis of on-demand ride-hailing systems	Ride-sourcing	Efficiency	No overarching differences in average waiting time for customers of ride-sourcing and traditional taxis. Maintaining or regulating either, depending on context, can be justified
Aarhaug and Olsen (2018)	Implications of ride-sourcing and self-driving vehicles on the need for regulation in unscheduled passenger transport	Ride-sourcing	Market	Shared and autonomous mobility will hurt taxis the most. New regulations are required to ensure that these new mobility options are fare and effective
Posen (2015)	Ride-sharing in the sharing economy: Should regulators impose Uber regulations on Uber	Ride-sourcing	Market/reg.	Existing mobility regulation is outdated. Experimental regulations will allow for effective evaluations and increased customer choice
Basu et al. (2018)	Automated Mobility-on-Demand vs Mass Transit: A Multi-Modal Activity-Driven Agent-Based Simulation Approach	Ride-sourcing	Modality	Automated mobility-on-demand will continue to challenge mass transit for ridership, but the latter is indispensable for effective and sustainable urban mobility
Hall et al. (2018)	Is Uber a substitute or complement for public transit?	Ride-sourcing	Modality Congestion	Uber acts as a feeder system that contributes to increase public transit ridership, especially for small transit agencies and rail services, but also increases and net commute time and may still contribute to increased congestion

Continued

Table 1 Literature on shared automobility.—Cont'd

Article	Title	Type of sharing	Theme/criteria	General findings, notes
Sadowsky and Nelson (2017)	The impact of ride-hailing services on public transportation use: A discontinuity regression analysis	Ride-sourcing	Modality	Evidence suggests that presence of single service complements transit by serving as a feeder and last mile solution; when there are two, they compete with and substitute transit
Brazil and Kirk (2016)	Uber and Metropolitan Traffic Fatalities in the United States	Ride-sourcing	Public health	For aggregate and drunk-driving instances, Uber has had no measurable impact on the number of traffic fatalities. Popular claims of such benefits are without empirical basis
Dills and Mulholland (2018)	Ride-Sharing, Fatal Crashes, and Crime	Ride-sourcing	Public health	Presence of Uber associated with reduction in DUI and fatal accidents, and in some instances, arrests for assault and disorderly conduct; and an increase in vehicle thefts
Greenwood and Wattal (2017)	Show Me the Way to Go Home: An Empirical Investigation of Ride-Sharing and Alcohol Related Motor Vehicle Fatalities	Ride-sourcing	Public health	Uber X associated with significant reduction in alcohol-related fatalities. No such relationship for Uber Black. Impact takes 1 year to manifest and does not hold during surge pricing
Martin-Buck (2017)	Responsible options: empirical analyses on the effects of alternative transportation on drunk driving	Ride-sourcing	Public health	Ride-sourcing "reduces fatal alcohol-related auto accidents by 10–11.4%." Cities with lower levels of transit service experienced greater reductions

Morrison et al. (2017)	Ride-sharing and Motor Vehicle Crashes in four US Cities: An Interrupted Time-Series Analysis	Ride-sourcing	Public health	Despite local variations, Uber's market entry and resumption after absence has been shown to reduce alcohol-related crash fatalities and have no effect on non-alcohol-related crashes
Peck (2017)	New York City Drunk Driving After Uber	Ride-sourcing	Public health	Implied decrease in collisions of 25–35% with greatest effects in densely populated areas
Mishra and Clewlow (2017)	Disruptive transportation: The adoption, utilization, and impacts of ride-hailing in the United States	Ride-sourcing	Users Modality	Users are younger and more educated, and motivated by lack of parking and avoiding drunk driving. Competes with most public transit with 6% net reduction, but complements commuter rail, which saw 3% increase

technologies and business practices; companies would do well to actively work with authorities to develop the sort of regulatory frameworks that would ensure the success of sharing economy platforms (Cannon and Summers, 2014). Examples of steps that can be taken include regulatory classification, licensing requirements, data sharing and even the provision of infrastructure.

In terms of classification, most ride-sourcing platforms are eager to be categorized as communications platforms rather than transportation network companies, let alone a transportation provider. In Vienna, for example, Uber has confronted challenges as it has at different times been classified as a rental car company as well as a taxi company. The classification of the drivers matters as well—when they are considered to be workers, as opposed to independent contractors, they are more likely to be protected by labor regulations (Zou, 2017). New York City, on the other hand, circumvents organizational classification by focusing on the vehicles, which are legally considered "for hire vehicles." In order to operate a (dynamic) ride-sourcing vehicle in NYC, a driver must obtain commercial license plates as well as commercial automobile insurance. Furthermore, the city has placed a cap of 80,000 on the number of such licenses that will be given out—it's worth noting though that this dwarfs the cap of 13,537 on NYC's iconic yellow cabs (Laurie, 2019). In some instances, local governments and regulators can facilitate the upscaling of certain forms of shared automobility deemed to be beneficial. In Oslo, for example, the municipal authorities have begun offering car sharing companies exclusive rights to a limited number of public parking spaces in the hopes that it encourages more use from people who would have otherwise owned their own car.

Shared automobility will shine a brighter light on the role of local governments in urban transport. In terms of who gets to do the regulations, Davidson and Infranca (2016) argue that unlike previous transportation disruptions, which have disproportionately been determined by national governments, the changes associated with shared mobility are urban and nature, and as such, should involve more active roles for municipal authorities. Rauch and Schleicher (2015) argue that once the dust settles from the ongoing series of litigation between various governments and start-ups, local and state government will likely begin cooperating, promoting, and in some instances, contracting with the new companies to deliver public services.

Another way in which to regulate shared automobility, and all automobility in urban areas for that matter, is road pricing and parking regulations. If shared automobility will also be autonomous, then "roadway pricing or other demand-management policies may well be needed, to avoid excessive AV use and worsened roadway congestion" (Fagnant and Kockelman, 2018). Although measures like congestion pricing and parking removal are ways to regulate car use without the legal hassles concerning classification and labor laws, the opposition that they tend to draw from local and nearby residents often makes such approaches politically toxic.

5.2 Blurring the boundaries between shared automobility modes

The technological foundation upon which sharing economy platforms rest have enabled transactional relationships with a wider network of actors, mostly importantly, among strangers. For decades, these transactions had been reserved for informal arrangements among close networks of family and friends. Given the pace of technological innovation it should be expected that these transactional relationships will change in the coming years.

Of the three forms of shared automobility discussed in this chapter, carpooling was the first, mostly because it did not require an ICT interface to allow consumers to grant each other temporary access to under-utilized physical assets—for decades, HOV lanes were enough. It is, however, the smartphone and internet connectivity that are at the root of carpooling's rise in availability and popularity after years of decline. The new form of carpooling, often referred to as dynamic ride-sharing, marks an overlap between the ride-sharing and the ride-sourcing modes. These two modes show signs of consolidation whereby most trips will involve multiple passengers sharing a vehicles and single-passenger trips being reserved only for those willing to pay a premium. The dynamic nature of the boundaries between the three forms of shared automobility do not stop here though.

For now, car sharing remains distinct from ride-sharing and ride-sourcing because it is the only one of the three modes that involves a user operated vehicle. This applies to both P2P car sharing, which exemplifies the sharing economy, as well as traditional B2C car sharing, which is more representative of its cousin—the business-service economy. If and when autonomous vehicles become more mainstream, or even dominant, an automobile would be able to drop off one passenger and pick another one up without needing to park and wait, effectively eliminating the distinction between car sharing and dynamic ride-sharing/sourcing.

Autonomous vehicles have the potential to consolidate all three modes of shared automobility. If this were to happen, then shared automobility would function very similarly to a type of shared mobility that already exists today, namely, micro-transit, which "serve passengers using dynamically generated routes...(and)...provide transit-like service but on a smaller, more flexible scale" (SUMC, 2015). Enoch (2015) describes this as a "modal convergence into a universal automated taxi service" that can be the dominant form or urban transportation in the future, replacing not only cars, but also taxis and busses. The merging among different types of shared automobility will have huge implications, but with like with other forms of shared mobility, any benefits will depend on the extent of sharing (Shaheen and Cohen, 2018).

5.3 Autonomous fleets and their urban implications

The future of shared automobility will depend a great deal on the extent to which it is automated. The Society of Automotive Engineers (SAE) defines six levels of automation with respect to the extent to which the human driver or machine is in control of the vehicle. Level zero is a fully manual vehicle with no automation, whereas level five involves full automation for steering, acceleration, deceleration, and other monitoring and feedback systems. According to the SAE, we do not need to wait for level five (i.e., 100% automation) to start replacing our current vehicle fleets, and even some public transit modes.

Some manufacturers and urban transport operators leapfrogging levels two or three, which involve partial or conditional automation; such levels rely on cooperation and sharing of responsibilities between the driver and machine, and can lead to potentially dangerous situations in which the driver thinks the car is in autonomous mode when it is not (Nenseth et al., 2019). Level four allow for vehicles without pedals and steering wheels that can operate as local driverless taxis (SAE, 2014) and public transit with fixed and scheduled routes that are segregated from other traffic (Nenseth et al., 2019).

Despite the potential to use autonomous vehicles in urban transit systems, Enoch (2015) cites rail-based transport, both in large urban areas and for long-distance routes, as modes that would continue to be advantageous in an autonomous age; however, it may be difficult to mobilize the resources needed to invest in rail when competing against shared autonomous fleets. Fagnant and Kockelman (2018) go further when pointing out that the convenience of private low-occupancy autonomous vehicles may be such that they may end up undercutting public mass transit, and even private high-occupancy vehicles and active transit. As Martinez and Viegas (2017) argue, an equitable urban mobility system that has a high level of automation must rest upon a foundation of mass transit (i.e., metro rail) and walkability. If autonomous vehicles end up competing with, rather than complementing, public mass transit, that foundation can crumble.

The Institute of Transport Economics in Norway envisions five scenarios for autonomous vehicles use in the country (Nenseth et al., 2019):

1. "Individual AVs for all: Unrestricted individual mobility by driverless cars
2. Curbed congestion: Restricted urban car use, i.e., few private AVs in cities
3. AVs in Carsharing: Optimized use of urban space by giving up the private car
4. AVs in Ride-sharing: Seamless, individualized flexible microtransport by MaaS
5. Automated public transport: Prioritized scheduled high-frequent AV public transport"

The first scenario based on private ownership and use resulted in significant urban congestion. The second scenario, also based on private ownership and consumption did not result in congestion, but only because it was assumed that there would be regulations to restrict vehicle access to and use within cities. The remaining scenarios all resulted in no urban congestion, but only when assuming that passengers were engaging in ride-sharing.

5.4 Impacts of shared automobility

Scholarship on the three modes of shared automobility tend to focus on different themes. The ride-sharing literature was the earliest to emerge and was generally interested in why carpooling was in decline and whether HOV lanes could increase the practice so as to alleviate road congestion during rush hour. Although HOV lanes were shown to be effective, carpooling remained a marginal practice in the broader mobility context. Congestion is the most prominent theme within the literature on ride-sharing and ride-sourcing. In almost all cases, ride-sharing as carpooling delivered reductions in net environmental benefits. The only exception to this is if carpooling attracts mobility users that were formerly public transit riders, which is certainly possible considering the potential cost reductions associated with autonomous vehicles.

The discussion over modality is also prominent in the shared automobility literature. The general agreement among researchers is that walking, bicycling and public transit are the sustainable modes of mobility. The relationship between shared automobility and these other modes largely depends on context and competitiveness of these other modes therein.

What appears to be unanimous in the literature is that despite the nuances of competitiveness and complementarity, any future urban mobility system that relies on shared automobility must also have robust and effective public transit and active transit options.

Given that the costs of traditional automobility are increasingly apparent and that local governments throughout the world are working to mitigate and/or avoid these costs, it may seem surprising that new ways of using the automobile, rather than getting rid of them, may actually help solve many of these problems.

On the one hand, shared mobility is part of the traditional system of automobility. It distinguishes itself, however, from the traditional variety by eliminating the private ownership and use of the vehicle. Similarly, shared automobility is related to the overall sharing economy but distinguishes itself from other innovative mobility solutions like bike and scooter sharing platforms. When compared with these other forms of shared mobility, shared automobility has an advantage in that it builds off of the dominant logic of the incumbent mobility system which has been designed for automobile use. Equipping cities to accommodate increased bicycling and public transit use may require building new infrastructure and disrupting the material foundations of urban areas. Shared automobility, on the other hand, relies more on new software and technology to enable new types of automobile use within urban infrastructure that is quite like the one we already have.

The potential rise of autonomous vehicles also has large public health implications. Automobile accidents result in over 1 million deaths, the majority of whom are pedestrians and cyclists, per year worldwide; it is the tenth leading cause of death in the world and the leading cause of injury-related death (WHO, 2016). The public health impact of shared automobility has been addressed most noticeably in the literature on ride-sourcing and dynamic ride-sharing. The majority of these studies focus on the effects of these new mobility options on the prevalence of accidents while driving under the influence of alcohol. The introduction of autonomous vehicles, which are not subject to human error or substance abuse, would significantly reduce road fatalities and injuries. There has, however, been very little research carried out on the public health impacts of car sharing and the effects of shared automobility on local pollution.

5.5 Further research

Shared automobility modes are not static categories. They have already exhibited signs of consolidation and may consolidate further. Their relationship to each other and other modes of transportation is crucial. As such, we need to focus more on the link between shared automobility and multimodal urban transportation and mobility as a service. We, furthermore, need broader long-term and multi-context studies to understand the temporal and geographic particularities of shared automobility.

With respect to environmental impact, most of the studies use VKT and vehicle holdings as the primary indicators. While this is useful, it paints an incomplete picture giving less emphasis to non-carbon emissions like nitrous oxide, carbon monoxide that are not associated with VKT as compared with carbon dioxide. Future research should incorporate these other harmful emissions to provide a more comprehensive account of environmental impact. Furthermore, as the proportion of battery-electric and other zero-emissions vehicles on the roads increases, it would be worthwhile to pay more attention to levels of suspended particulate matter (SPM) which are a leading cause of respiratory harm among urban residents (Uherek et al., 2010). If shared automobility reduced net VKT but increases it in urban pockets, the health costs could be dramatic. In general, the environmental footprint of shared mobility services, especially those that involve cars, is currently understood based on assumptions and uncertainties. Future research should seek to apply more complex and complete ways of analyzing its impacts, e.g., through life cycle assessments (LCAs).

The emergence of autonomous vehicles has the potential to transform shared automobility even further. As the technology and its use becomes more prevalent, it must be incorporated into research on shared automobility, especially in instances in which it blurs the boundaries between car sharing and the other two modes. And furthermore, as autonomous shared automobility may compete with public transit, the relationship between the two deserves more attention.

Short term impacts in relation to congestion have been well-studied, which is not to suggest that there is no longer a need to improve our understanding of the effects of shared automobility on urban mobility. The study of the longer-term impacts on urban land form have been less active. On the one hand, this is understandable considering how recent shared automobility is. On the other hand, it has been around for at least a decade now and the time is ripe to begin considering the implications of ride-sourcing, ride-sharing and car sharing on land use, in terms of both policy as well as demographic trends.

When considered in an automobility context, the automobile has been associated with decades of sprawl characterized by segregated functionality, single family homes, central business districts and controlled access motorways connecting them all. For many, sprawl is a shorthand for such land use practices. Shared automobility provides new ways of living and working in urban areas that directly challenge the logic of sprawl.

But the impacts of shared automobility surely extends beyond this even. We have only begun to scratch the surface of the cultural and social implications of shared automobility. What will be the impact of shared automobility if and when vehicles are autonomous? How will this shape the often segregated school districts found in and around urban areas. Will suburbanization continue, not just in terms of land use but in terms of culture? And then there are the impacts on shopping malls, strip malls, elderly homes, assisted living, business parks, knowledge clusters, labor mobility, immigration, segregation, conceptualizations of masculinity, status, freedom, sustainability—the list of potential parameters is endless.

Acknowledgment

This chapter is a product of the following research project, and we are grateful to *The Research Council of Norway* (www.nfr.no) for supporting this study: TEMPEST project, funded by ENERGIX-program, The Research Council of Norway https://www.toi.no/tempest/

References

Aarhaug, J., Olsen, S., 2018. Implications of ride-sourcing and self-driving vehicles on the need for regulation in unscheduled passenger transport. Res. Transp. Econ. 69, 573–582.

Agatz, N., Erera, A., Savelsbergh, M., Wang, X., 2012. Optimization for dynamic ride-sharing: a review. Eur. J. Oper. Res. 223 (2), 295–303.

Albino, V., Berardi, U., Dangelico, R.M., 2015. Smart cities: definitions, dimensions, performance, and initiatives. J. Urban Technol. 22 (1), 3–21.

Albinsson, P.A., Perera, B.Y., 2018. The Rise of the Sharing Economy: Exploring the Challenges and Opportunities of Collaborative Consumption. Praeger, Santa Barbera, California.

Banister, D., 2008. The sustainable mobility paradigm. Transp. Policy 15 (2), 73–80.

Baptista, P., Melo, S., Rolim, C., 2014. Energy, environmental and mobility impacts of car-sharing systems. Empirical results from Lisbon, Portugal. Procedia Soc. Behav. Sci. 111, 28–37.

Basu, R., Araldo, A., Akkinepally, A.P., Nahmias Biran, B.H., Basak, K., Seshadri, R., … Ben-Akiva, M., 2018. Automated mobility-on-demand vs. mass transit: a multi-modal activity-driven agent-based simulation approach. Transp. Res. Rec. 2672, 608–618. 0361198118758630.

Becker, U.J., Becker, T., Gerlach, J., 2012. The True Costs of Automobility: External Costs of Cars Overview on Existing Estimates in EU-27. Technische Universitat Dresden; Dresden.

Becker, H., Ciari, F., Axhausen, K.W., 2017. Comparing car-sharing schemes in Switzerland: user groups and usage patterns. Transp. Res. A Policy Pract. 97, 17–29.

Belk, R., 2010. Sharing. J. Consum. Res. 36, 715–734.

Beuren, F.H., Ferreira, M.G.G., Miguel, P.A.C., 2013. Product-service systems: a literature review on integrated products and services. J. Clean. Prod. 47, 222–231.

Brazil, N., Kirk, D.S., 2016. Uber and metropolitan traffic fatalities in the United States. Am. J. Epidemiol. 184 (3), 192–198.

Briceno, T., Peters, G., Solli, C., Hertwich, E., 2005. Using Life Cycle Approaches to Evaluate Sustainable Consumption Programs: Car-Sharing. .
Cannon, S., Summers, L.H., 2014. How Uber and the sharing economy can win over regulators. Harv. Bus. Rev. 13 (10), 24–28.
Cervero, R., 2003. City CarShare: first-year travel demand impacts. Transp. Res. Rec. 1839, 159–166.
Cervero, R., Tsai, Y., 2004. City CarShare in San Francisco, California: second-year travel demand and car ownership impacts. Transp. Res. Rec. 1887, 117–127.
Cervero, R., Golub, A., Nee, B., 2007. City CarShare: longer-term travel demand and car ownership impacts. Transp. Res. Rec. 1992, 70–80.
Chen, T.D., Kockelman, K.M., 2016. Carsharing's life-cycle impacts on energy use and greenhouse gas emissions. Transp. Res. Part D: Transp. Environ. 47, 276–284.
Cohen, B., Kietzmann, J., 2014. Ride on! Mobility business models for the sharing economy. Organ. Environ. 27 (3), 279–296.
Davidson, N.M., Infranca, J.J., 2016. The sharing economy as an urban phenomenon. Yale Law Policy Rev. 34, 215.
Dills, A.K., Mulholland, S.E., 2018. Ride-sharing, fatal crashes, and crime. South. Econ. J. 84 (4), 965–991.
Doka, G., Ziegler, S., 2001. Complete Life Cycle Assessment for Vehicle Models of the Mobility Carsharing Fleet Switzerland. In: Presented at the 1st Swiss Transport Research Conference. Ascona, Switzerland.
Enoch, M.P., 2015. How a rapid modal convergence into a universal automated taxi service could be the future for local passenger transport. Tech. Anal. Strat. Manag. 27 (8), 910–924.
Fagnant, D.J., Kockelman, K.M., 2018. Dynamic ride-sharing and fleet sizing for a system of shared autonomous vehicles in Austin, Texas. Transportation 45 (1), 143–158.
Feng, G., Kong, G., Wang, Z., 2017. We are on the way: analysis of on-demand ride-hailing systems. SSRN Electron. J. https://doi.org/10.2139/ssrn.2960991.
Ferguson, E., 1997. The rise and fall of the American carpool: 1970–1990. Transportation 24 (4), 349–376.
Firnkorn, J., Müller, M., 2011. What will be the environmental effects of new free-floating car-sharing systems? The case of car2go in Ulm. Ecol. Econ. 70 (8), 1519–1528.
Frenken, K., Schor, J., 2017. Putting the sharing economy into perspective. Environ. Innov. Soc. Trans. 23, 3–10.
Frenken, K., Meelen, T., Arets, M., van de Glind, P., 2015. Smarter Regulation for the Sharing Economy. The Guardian, p. 20.
Fukuyama, F., 2011. The Origins of Political Order: From Prehuman Times to the French Revolution. Farrar, Straus and Giroux.
Geels, F., Kemp, R., Dudley, G., Lyons, G., 2011. Automobility in Transition?: A Socio-Technical Analysis of Sustainable Transport. Routledge.
George, C., Julsrud, T.E., 2018. The Development of Organised Car Sharing in Norway: 1995–2018. Retrieved from, https://www.toi.no/getfile.php?mmfileid=49603.
Greenwood, B.N., Wattal, S., 2017. Show me the way to go home: an empirical investigation of ride-sharing and alcohol related motor vehicle fatalities. MIS Q. 41 (1), 163–187.
Gruszka, K., 2017. Framing the collaborative economy—voices of contestation. Environ. Innov. Soc. Trans. 23, 92–104.
Hall, J.D., Palsson, C., Price, J., 2018. Is Uber a substitute or complement for public transit? J. Urban Econ. 108, 36–50.
Harms, S., Truffer, B., 1998. The emergence of a nation-wide carsharing co-operative in Switzerland. In: A Case-Study for the EC-Supported Research Project "Strategic Niche Management as a Tool for Transition to a Sustainable Transport System". EAWAG, Zürich.

Hertwich, E.G., 2005. Consumption and the rebound effect: an industrial ecology perspective. J. Ind. Ecol. 9 (1–2), 85–98.
Ingold, T., 1986. The appropriation of nature. In: Essays on Human Ecology and Social Relations. Manchester University Press, Manchester.
Javid, R.J., Nejat, A., Salari, M., 2016. The environmental impacts of carpooling in the United States. In: Paper Presented at the Proceedings of the Transportation, Land and Air Quality Conference.
Javid, R.J., Nejat, A., Hayhoe, K., 2017. Quantifying the environmental impacts of increasing high occupancy vehicle lanes in the United States. Transp. Res. Part D: Transp. Environ. 56, 155–174.
Jittrapirom, P., Caiati, V., Feneri, A.-M., Ebrahimigharehbaghi, S., Alonso González, M.J., Narayan, J., 2017. Mobility as a service: a critical review of definitions, assessments of schemes, and key challenges. Urban Plan. 2, 13–25.
Jorge, D., Correia, G., 2013. Carsharing systems demand estimation and defined operations: a literature review. Eur. J. Transp. Infrastruct. Res. 13 (3), 201–220.
Katzev, R., 1999. Carsharing Portland: Review and Analysis of its First Year. Department of Environmental Quality, Portland, Ore.
Lane, C., 2005. PhillyCarShare: first-year social and mobility impacts of carsharing in Philadelphia, Pennsylvania. Transp. Res. Rec. 1927, 158–166.
Laurie, K.A., 2019. Capping Uber in new York City: ramifications for rideshares, the road, and outer-borough residents. Fordham Urban Law J. 46 (4), 942.
Lessig, L., 2008. Remix: Making Art and Commerce Thrive in the Hybrid Economy. Penguin.
Li, Z., Hong, Y., Zhang, Z., 2016a. Do ride-sharing services affect traffic congestion? An empirical study of Uber entry. Soc. Sci. Res. Netw. 2002, 1–29.
Li, Z., Hong, Y., Zhang, Z., 2016b. An empirical analysis of on-demand ride sharing and traffic congestion. In: International Conference on Information Systems 2016. Dublin, Ireland from December 11–14.
Loose, W., 2010. The state of European car-sharing. In: Project Momo Final Report D, 2.
Lyons, G., 2018. Getting smart about urban mobility—aligning the paradigms of smart and sustainable. Transp. Res. A Policy Pract. 115, 4–14.
Malhotra, A., Van Alstyne, M., 2014. The dark side of the sharing economy… and how to lighten it. Commun. ACM 57 (11), 24–27.
Martin, C.J., 2016. The sharing economy: a pathway to sustainability or a nightmarish form of neoliberal capitalism? Ecol. Econ. 121, 149–159.
Martin, E.W., Shaheen, S.A., 2011. Greenhouse gas emission impacts of carsharing in North America. IEEE Trans. Intell. Transp. Syst. 12 (4), 1074–1086.
Martin, E., Shaheen, S.A., Lidicker, J., 2010. Impact of carsharing on household vehicle holdings: results from north American shared-use vehicle survey. Transp. Res. Rec. 2143 (1), 150–158.
Martin-Buck, F.P., 2017. Responsible Options: Empirical Analyses on the Effects of Alternative Transportation on Drunk Driving. University of Texas; Austin.
Martinez, L.M., Viegas, J.M., 2017. Assessing the impacts of deploying a shared self-driving urban mobility system: an agent-based model applied to the city of Lisbon, Portugal. Int. J. Transp. Sci. Technol. 6 (1), 13–27.
Meijkamp, R., 1998. Changing consumer behaviour through eco-efficient services: an empirical study of car sharing in the Netherlands. Bus. Strateg. Environ. 7 (4), 234–244.
Millard-Ball, A., 2005. Car-Sharing: Where and How it Succeeds. vol. 108 Transportation Research Board.
Minett, P., Pearce, J., 2011. Estimating the energy consumption impact of casual carpooling. Energies 4 (1), 126–139.

Mishra, G.S., Clewlow, R.R., 2017. Disruptive Transportation: The Adoption, Utilization, and Impacts of Ride-Hailing in the United States. University of California, Davis, Institute of Transportation Studies, Davis, CA. Research Report UCD-ITS-RR-17-07.

Morrison, C.N., Jacoby, S.F., Dong, B., Delgado, M.K., Wiebe, D.J., 2017. Ridesharing and motor vehicle crashes in 4 US cities: an interrupted time-series analysis. Am. J. Epidemiol. 187 (2), 224–232.

Nenseth, V., Ciccone, A., Kristensen, N.B., 2019. Societal Consequences of Automated Vehicles–Norwegian Scenarios. TØI Report. 1700/2019.

Nijland, H., van Meerkerk, J., 2017. Mobility and environmental impacts of car sharing in the Netherlands. Environ. Innov. Soc. Trans. 23, 84–91.

OED, 2019. Share, n.1. Oxford University Press.

Ou, H., Tang, T.-Q., 2018. Impacts of carpooling on trip costs under car-following model. Physica A 505, 136–143.

Peck, J.L., 2017. New York City Drunk Driving After Uber. CUNY Academic Works.

Posen, H.A., 2015. Ridesharing in the sharing economy: should regulators impose Uber regulations on Uber. Iowa Law Rev. 101, 405.

Price, J.A., 1975. Sharing: the integration of intimate economics. Antropologica 17 (1), 3–27.

Puschmann, T., Alt, R., 2016. Sharing economy. Bus. Inf. Syst. Eng. 58 (1), 93–99.

Rauch, D.E., Schleicher, D., 2015. Like Uber, but for local government law: the future of local regulation of the sharing economy. Ohio State Law J. 76, 901.

Reim, W., Parida, V., Örtqvist, D., 2015. Product–service systems (PSS) business models and tactics–a systematic literature review. J. Clean. Prod. 97, 61–75.

Sadowsky, N., Nelson, E., 2017. The Impact of Ride-Hailing Services on Public Transportation Use: A Discontinuity Regression Analysis. Bowdoin College, Economics Department (Working Paper Series).

SAE, 2014. Taxonomy and definitions for terms related to on-road motor vehicle automated driving systems. SAE Standard J. 3016, 1–16.

Schor, J., 2016. Debating the sharing economy. J. Self-Gov. Manag. Econ. 4 (3), 7–22.

Shaheen, S.A., Cohen, A.P., 2007. Growth in worldwide carsharing: an international comparison. Transp. Res. Rec. 1992 (1), 81–89.

Shaheen, S., Cohen, A., 2018. Shared ride services in North America: definitions, impacts, and the future of pooling. Transp. Rev. 39 (4), 427–442.

Shaheen, S., Stocker, A., 2015. Carsharing for Business, Zipcar Case Study & Impact Analysis (Information Brief). University of California Berkeley, Retrieved from http://innovativemobility.org/wpcontent/uploads/2015/07/Zipcar_Corporate_Final_v6.pdf.

Shaheen, S.A., Chan, N.D., Gaynor, T., 2016. Casual carpooling in the San Francisco Bay area: understanding user characteristics, behaviors, and motivations. Transp. Policy 51, 165–173.

Shaheen, S., Cohen, A., Bayen, A., 2018. The Benefits of Carpooling. UC Berkeley.

Sioui, L., Morency, C., Trépanier, M., 2013. How carsharing affects the travel behavior of households: a case study of Montréal, Canada. Int. J. Sustain. Transp. 7 (1), 52–69.

Steininger, K., Vogl, C., Zettl, R., 1996. Car-sharing organizations: the size of the market segment and revealed change in mobility behavior. Transp. Policy 3 (4), 177–185.

SUMC, 2015. Shared-Use Mobility-Reference Guide. Los Angeles, CA, Chicago.

Tinson, J., Nutall, P., 2008. Insider trading? Exploring familiar intra-generational borrowing and sharing. Eur. Adv. Consum. Res. 8, 41–42.

Uherek, E., Halenka, T., Borken-Kleefeld, J., Balkanski, Y., Berntsen, T., Borrego, C., … Lelieveld, J., 2010. Transport impacts on atmosphere and climate: land transport. Atmos. Environ. 44 (37), 4772–4816.

Urry, J., 2004. The 'system' of automobility. Theory Cult. Soc. 21 (4–5), 25–39.
Walb, C., Loudon, W., 1986. Evaluation of the Short-Term Auto Rental (STAR) Service in San Francisco. US Department of Transportation, Urban Mass Transportation Administration, CA.
Walks, A., 2014. The Urban Political Economy and Ecology of Automobility: Driving Cities, Driving Inequality, Driving Politics. Routledge.
WHO, 2016. Road Traffic Injuries Fact Sheet. World Health Organization, Geneva.
Zou, M., 2017. The regulatory challenges of 'Uberization' in China: classifying ride-hailing drivers. Int. J. Comp. Labour Law Ind. Relat. 33 (2), 269–294.

CHAPTER THREE

Public transport in a sharing environment

Wijnand Veeneman*
Delft University of Technology, Delft, The Netherlands
*Corresponding author: e-mail address: w.w.veeneman@tudelft.nl

Contents

Abstract

Shared modes can provide both a synergetic and a competitive relation with the existing public transport system. The competitive relation only is realistic when the shared modes have a positive business case. However, both with a positive and a negative business case, shared modes will operate in a mobility context with public authorities playing a major role in regulation and financing of services and infrastructure.

This chapter argues that this governmental role is key, and the challenge will be to strike a balance between allowing for innovation with shared modes and driving integration between all modes. That integration should put all modes in their strength and provide efficient integration between the different modes. Mobility as a service could to be an excellent tool for providing the integration, but public authorities could act on a wide set of policy fields, like infrastructure, spatial planning, public transport procurement, traffic regulation and more to tie shared services and public transport together. The outcome of the implementation of shared services for the larger mobility context relies highly on that successful integration.

Keywords: Shared mobility, Public transport, Governance, Business case, User perspective, Autonomous vehicles, Bike sharing, Integrated mobility

Advances in Transport Policy and Planning, Volume 4
ISSN 2543-0009
https://doi.org/10.1016/bs.atpp.2019.10.002

1. Introduction

The sharing economy and its role in transport has received a great deal of attention in recent years, especially due to the promise of Mobility as a Service (MaaS) to provide more integrated transport solutions (Standing et al., 2019). New forms of shared transport options are said to provide enhanced flexibility and more of a demand orientation compared to the original form of shared transport service, i.e., public transport, in which demand is combined in routes and vehicles. From its early inception to the late 1990s, policy makers, service providers and users alike distinguished two types of modes: private and public transport (Cervero, 2017).

Outside that dichotomy other modes exist, taxis and jitneys (Muñoz and Gschwender, 2008; Walters, 2008), also with sharing characteristics, but the academic debates seemed to focus on the tension between public transport with scheduled services on fixed lines and private transport, dedicated to the individuals or family transport needs. The key narrative around a great deal of research was focused on how public transport is needed to save us from the problems related to the car (Banister, 2008).

Both systems, car and public transport, have rather poor efficiencies. Cars are stationary more than 95% of the time CBS (2016) and filling the seats in public transport is also challenging. Even in public transport friendly environments, like major cities, highly directional peak flows (in and out of town) leave the seats of outbound trains empty in the morning and inbound trains empty in the evening (Parkinson and Fisher, 1996).

As the internet developed and platform economies emerged, it became clear that sharing the capacity of cars was highly promising. We saw platforms aimed at filling the many vacant seats in cars with low occupancy rates. We saw platforms aimed at sharing cars for people to drive themselves (see "Carsharing's impact and future" by Shaheen et al.). We saw platforms aimed at sharing an integrated transport service with cars, making them available and affordable taxi services. These platforms do nothing else than provide instant coordination of demand and supply of transport capacity through communication technology, allowing for new supply and demand to develop (see also "Sharing vehicles and sharing rides in real-time: Opportunities for self-driving fleets" by Gurumurthy et al.).

Also, for the bicycle, modern technologies simplified the coordination needed for shared use. Bike sharing gained traction since 2000 when large cities saw shared bikes becoming a mainstay of mobility, like the Paris *Velib*,

Barcelona's *Bicing* and New York *Citi Bike*, to free-floating bike sharing like the DB-bike in Germany. Later mainly Chinese and Singaporean entrepreneurs built on these models by making them real platform systems using the latest possibilities of the modern smartphone to find, book and pay for bikes (see also chapter "Bike share" by Fishman and Allan).

Because of the sharing of these vehicles, cars and bikes, that were originally typically private, the chasm between public and private was filled in a short period with many different transport services. Their growth was and is supported by private and public parties from different perspectives. Private parties provide a focus in individual use of service capacity and for profit (Litman, 2000). This does not necessarily provide a good outcome from a public perspective (see, for example, Li et al., 2016; Currie, 2018). For public parties, the focus is on shared use of vehicle including bike capacity and against congestion and emissions (see Wang and Zhou, 2017).

So, modern communication technology solves a coordination problem that had been existing for decades in private transport, with cars and bikes standing around most of the time. Sharing of vehicles and rides is simplified because of the ability to find, book and pay for the capacity, thus improving asset utilization, compared to if the private ownership model was the only means of access. The business case improved so much that new providers jumped on the bandwagon to establish themselves in this market.

And as technology moves forward again, with sensor and computational technology, and with electric propulsion, we are told that wide-spread introduction of self-driving electric vehicles is around the corner (see also "Sharing vehicles and sharing rides in real-time: Opportunities for self-driving fleets" by Gurumurthy et al.). Again, self-driving of vehicles could further shift the business model of a wide variety of transport modes, with staff costs dropping. CROW (2015) shows for the Dutch context that half of the cost of one bus hour is related to the driver. In addition, key costs of energy and staff will be dramatically reduced because of automation. Again, CROW expects a 75% reduction of energy costs. In a sharing context, the pinnacle seems to be capacity of vehicles as simply available as capacity of infrastructure: you do not own it, but it is ready for you when you step out the door. The literature is highly polarized on the expected effects of shared, self-driving electric vehicles in general (e.g., see Currie, 2018; Fagnant and Kockelman, 2015).

The space between traditional public and private transport is filling up with more hybrid forms of transport (see Table 1), hybrid in a sense that the combine characteristics of public and private modes. In this chapter

Table 1 Public shared and private transport services for personal mobility.

Transport service	Infrastructure	Vehicle	Driver	Locations and times[a]	Trips	Examples
Public	Dedicated	Service	Service	Scheduled lines	Combined	Train, metro, tram, some bus
	Shared	Service	Service	Scheduled lines	Combined	Bus, ferry, some tram
Shared	Shared	Driver owned	Driver traveler	Continuous	Combined	Ride sharing
	Shared	Driver owned	Service	Service hours	Dedicated	Ride hailing
	Shared	Service	Driver traveler	Continuous	Dedicated	Free roaming bike or scooter sharing
	Shared	Service	Driver traveler	Continuous	Dedicated	Car and bike rental and docked sharing
	Shared	Service	Service	Service hours	Combined	Jitney
	Shared	Service	Service	Continuous	Dedicated	Taxi
Private	Shared	Driver owned	Driver traveler	Continuous	Dedicated	Car, motorbike, bicycle, scooter

[a]Continuous is always dependent on possible erratic supply.
Source: Veeneman, W., Van Kuijk, J.I, Hiemstra-van Mastrigt, S., 2019. Dreaming of the travellers experience in 2040: exploring governance strategies and their consequences for personal mobility systems. In: Mueler, B. Meyer, G., Towards User Centric Transport. Springer.

we will look at the effect of new forms of shared mobility on public transport. Will car-sharing reduce public transport use as it will further enhance the value proposition of car based transport, making it more attractive and accessible? Will the traditional train be replaced by self-driving pods, on rails or on roads? Or will shared mobility fit nicely into the mix of existing modes and provide an alternative for just a few specific niches? What exactly that future is remains unclear, but here we will interpret the first signals this ongoing change is providing us.

This paper relies on research carried out at Delft University of Technology. Although the literature reviewed covers an international perspective, it has a bias toward the Netherlands. The country is known for transport innovation, as one of the pioneers of protected bike lanes, lower urban speed limits, electric vehicle policy, etc. Therefore, the Netherlands could provide a useful vantage point to examine what the future of public transport might look like in the age of disruptive transport innovation. Hence, many examples, hopefully inspiring, have a Dutch flavor. In the next section we will look at logistics, business, user and governance perspectives on the relation between shared modes and public transport, followed by discussion and conclusion.

2. Perspectives on public transport and shared and autonomous modes

2.1 Introduction

The debate on the impact of shared and self-driving vehicles on public transport has been going on for some time, with little empirical evidence and a broad set of outcomes in modeling approaches (see, for example, Walker, 2015). With the swift introduction of shared modes and the looming promise of autonomous driving vehicles, it seems that research has had a hard time keeping up on the more intricate analysis of the overall effects of these new modes on the existing. The expected effects are very much dependent on the perspective taken. Consequently, we will make a distinction between these different perspectives and go through the research available to provide a broad perspective on the possible interactions between public transport and the new modes.

2.2 A logistics perspective

In much of the literature public transport is seen as a mode on its own, expected to deliver the full range of transport services with near-by accessibility and long-distance reach. When we look at the literature of designing public transport systems (like van Nes et al., 1988; Vuchic, 2017), it emphasizes that it is a layered system, with higher and lower operational speeds and capacities. The slower modes provide accessibility to the total system, with design rules placing bus stops around 500 m from every front door. The faster modes provide speed for the overall system, with high speed trains traveling at up to 500 kph. Obviously, the traveler will have to transfer between systems to have an accessible and fast system. Many systems were designed to provide just that, to provide a complete alternative for the car to create a modal shift.

Over the years, it became clear that car and public transport can serve different needs, even in a single trip chain, and, if well-integrated, can provide an excellent combined service. Park and Ride and Kiss and Ride became part of the transport system designer's idiom. They show how integration of these modes requires facilities (Noel, 1988; Parkhurst, 2000). A smooth transfer between the two is essentially making both modes better. In addition, bicycle and public transport proved to be a very effective combination when the bicycle infrastructure connects with the train system, such as in the Netherlands, where 50% of train travelers arrive at the station by bike (KIM, 2018). Again, this requires facilities to park bikes and allow users to easily transfer between the two modes (see also Kager et al., 2016).

Logistically, it is somewhat of a challenge to couple private free-floating transport to public scheduled and routed services. For example, car driving is not scheduled, and arrival times have a lot of variation, depending on the congestion the driver is encountering. Scheduled services are, in well designed and operated systems, intended to provide easy transfers and operated to secure these connections, for example, between busses and trains. Free-floating modes, like cars, have less predictable arrival times, with the need for more slack in travel times. Moreover, we find intercity stations mostly in dense urban areas, to cater to the high levels of demand. Parking space in dense urban areas is expensive and accessibility to these places congested, again making the link between car and train challenging. Finally, most travelers find it easier to access the departure station by bike or car, but you generally do not have one at your arrival station, except for those using folding bikes. The combination of car and train provides issues in securing the logistical coordination (Arendsen, 2019).

In both forms of modal integration (or transit fusion, see Currie, 2018), public transport with car and with bike, sharing has made an impact. As the last example above shows, the logistical advantage of sharing modes is high on the station of arrival. Here it can provide travelers alternative last mile solutions to slower public transport routes. We see bike sharing taking a place in this last mile challenge. In the Netherlands, access on bicycle to train transport has been traditionally high, with the Dutch owning more bikes than it has inhabitants. Egress using bicycles has been growing, due to shared bike systems. This happened first with OV-fiets, linked to Dutch rail and available almost exclusively at train stations. Later the free-floating bikes were added to that and provided an additional alternative to integrate cycling with public transport (Boor, 2019; Janmaat, 2019).

The effect of ride hailing on public transport use for now does not seem to develop into the direction of transit fusion in the combination of the qualities of train and car. A study in Santiago de Chile analyzed ride-hailing and its relation to public transport travel. The study showed a ratio of 11 to 1, 11 ride hails substituting public transport to 1 combining public transport and ride hailing inefficiencies (Tirachini and del Río, 2019).

The traditional hybrid between public and private transport, the taxi, can illustrate a key problem of linking shared systems like ride hailing and locations of high demand like stations. Many larger stations have taxi ranks. The rank itself makes the efficiency obvious. Inefficiencies are less obvious in ride hailing, where waiting is more distributed. However, ranks located in areas of high demand provide direct availability of the service and this is of great value. And although there is visible inefficiency in the waiting, that direct availability still seems to be a strong point of the taxi, compared to ride hailing.

The link between car sharing and public transport is somewhat less straightforward. On the one hand we see authorities promote car sharing, with a tendency to develop mobility hubs where all modes come together. Also, railway operators like Dutch rail support car sharing, with cars provided at stations. But Arendsen (2019) shows that the shared car plays a much smaller role in access and egress to train services. Car sharing is in itself more competitive to train services than bike or ride sharing.

The examples above show that the way in which shared and public transport modes integrate in terms of logistics is highly dependent on the spatial environment. In dense areas, capacity of infrastructure, vehicles and space in general is under constant pressure. Shared modes could provide value in these locations by enhancing the space efficiency of transport. However, that is very much dependent on occupancy and currently highly contested. In less densely populated areas, we see that sharing takes on a different role. In the Netherlands, transport authorities are actively seeking ways to supplant bus services for shared modes. The traditional bus service simply requires a higher level of demand than is available to support high occupancies the majority of the time. Some shared services are run with small busses that run on demand, often run by volunteers. Many transit agencies are also looking at self-driving vehicles. Also bike sharing is used to increase first and last mile options in less dense areas. Bike sharing can help to increase the catchment of public transport services significantly, as a bicycle can move at four times the speed of a pedestrian, increasing the catchment area by a factor of 15 (Hudson et al., 1982). An interesting example is provided by Arriva in the Netherlands, offering bike share in the trains (so not on stations) in those areas where demand for bike sharing is limited. The bikes are available on board the train. In these less dense areas, the sharing modes provide not so much a capacity advantage, but a clear cost advantage.

Logistically, the strength of the link between public transport and shared modes depends heavily on the network effect. When the shared mode is connected well to the existing public transport network, like with bike share at stations and on taxi ranks, the value of both systems increases. When the shared mode is developed more as a stand-alone transport service, it has a more competitive character.

There is one logistical challenge that plays an important part in the interaction between car and ride sharing on the one hand and public transport on the other. Shared modes offer strong gains in terms of capacity of vehicles, infrastructure and space over non-shared modes. But the capacity (Currie, 2018) of existing public transport in cities is still so much higher than what the e-hailing cars (e.g., Uber) can offer in a limited amount of space. A thousand seat train every 2 min or bus rapid transit every 30 s both offer up to 30,000 seats per hour on a specific link, about the maximum capacity of public transit can offer. Ride and car sharing mostly serves only one passenger per vehicle. This means that up to 30,000 vehicles per hour could be needed for the same demand. As cities become denser, the use of e-hailing car users as a replacement for public transport threatens to exacerbate traffic congestion issues. For interurban transport, coordinated automated vehicles could help, but would rely on all vehicles within the fleet to have the ability to communicate with one another. Moreover, for urban driving, it is unlikely vehicle to vehicle communication will provide the efficiency promised for highway driving.

We can expect that what is true for the current shared modes is probably also true for more advanced shared modes. When focusing on the car, autonomous cars could offer further savings of space and cost compared to current e-hailing and car share offerings (see "Carsharing's impact and future" by Shaheen et al. and "Sharing vehicles and sharing rides in real-time: Opportunities for self-driving fleets" by Gurumurthy et al.). They are anticipated to park themselves out of the way when not needed and they will not need a driver. The effect they have on public transport could be even stronger, for the good or for the bad. When well connected the two may be able to strengthen each other, by providing a convenient first mile/last mile solution. However, when developed in competition, public transport might lose value as the so-called *robo-taxi* may offer door-to-door convenience, at a price comparable to public transport. The business models and government environment related to optimizing the outcomes for emerging shared transport technology is briefly discussed in the following section.

2.3 A business perspective

As discussed above, shared transport services are expected to provide space savings and cost savings. The space savings are expected with regard to existing private modes, the cost savings with respect to existing public modes. Hence, those cost savings are interesting in the interaction between shared modes and public transport. The cost recovery of public transport is an important indicator for transport authorities providing transport services in their area (Hirschhorn et al., 2018). For authorities, it might be undesirable to spend tax revenue on running empty busses, but these busses are often seen as needed to provide the sense of spatial and temporal availability that public transport needs to be attractive. From an equity perspective, authorities quite reasonably want to provide sufficient coverage to connect all communities within their jurisdiction. From an economic reductionist/business perspective, offering services in areas with low demand is need as undesirable, but have been justified on equity grounds. In peri-urban areas and other locations with demand, smaller scale, demand responsive shared use vehicles may offer cost savings, as well as better emissions performance, but authorities must be cautious not to achieve an outcome whereby traditional public transport services are eroded in areas in which they are better suited than small scale, on demand services.

Here the lower (expected) costs of shared services make them attractive for authorities, to use them for those areas and times when demand is lower. This allows the authorities to focus the existing scheduled services on those routes where demand is high and provide demand responsive services that are providing shared rides in lieu of poorly used bus services. In the Netherlands, we have seen authorities use this tactic with great success (Veeneman et al., 2018). In Groningen and Drenthe bus services were made more direct, with higher operating speeds and frequencies, and lower stop density. Demand responsive services were integrated more in public transport to fill the gaps left along the old routes of the bus services. This led to growth of patronage on these lines up to 30% over 5 years. In the Amsterdam area the authority asked operators to include shared services into their supply to travelers, from the same perspective. Although the offer from the operator was promising, implementation issues prevented this example from reaching the same kinds of growth (Veeneman et al., 2019).

The above two cases provide examples of public transport authorities being in control of transport services through tendered concessions and driving the change toward the use of shared services. Here, the authorities can decide what services to procure, and whether to include demand responsive and shared modes into the concession. This is similar in large parts of Europe, South America, Asia and Australia. Governance will be discussed below.

But for some shared modes the business case can already be positive in itself, with ramifications for the role of authorities toward these shared modes. Or even with operational losses, private parties are rolling out the services to have the first-mover advantage (see also Wirtz and Tang, 2016). We see examples of providers of shared services moving in without the coordinating efforts of the transport operators. Bike sharing started in many countries as an improved form of bicycle renting, with better ease of access and availability, and the ability to end the hire period at your destination, rather than returning the bike to the pick up location (see also Boor, 2019; Fishman, 2016; Janmaat, 2019).

How strong this effect of a positive business case could be is something the Paris electric scooters could give us a glimpse of. The scooters are often faster and more comfortable to ride than bikes. They take up little space in the city and are not congesting the streets very quickly. Especially for shorter distances they can be faster than public transport, including the metro. This is quite a feat when traveling in a large city. *If* those shared systems can develop a true positive business case, for current operations or when they have dominated the market, the situation really changed from the above described two Dutch cases. It is not clear whether these shared modes will ultimately compete or complement traditional public transport. These shared services could act as door to door substitutes for traditional public transport. However, this still depends of a wide range of factors (Bakker, 2018), including the travelers' perspective on how they want to travel (something we will discuss below). Clearly, for the longer distances the scooters are not competitive, and prices are higher. In addition, authorities do occasionally step in and curtail these solutions (again discussed below), like in the Netherlands (Arendsen, 2019).

These examples show how with a positive business case, the link between shared modes and public transport can change dramatically. In this situation, authorities are not the ones asking for these services, which removes their agency for demanding specific implementation and hampers planning for the way in which shared modes are linked to other services. With the demonstrated market appetite from the commercial bike share sector to provide free-floating bike share without government subsidy, these systems often appeared without any discussion/agreement from city government. The same could happen with free-floating self-driving car services, and given the far larger footprint of cars, are likely to cause a dramatic increase in congestion without government regulation that anticipates and addresses this plausible impact. Linking them to existing public transport services becomes less of a positive action within a concession environment, as seen in the Dutch cases. The future success autonomous shared vehicles integrating successfully as a MaaS system will depend more on the interplay between market forces and regulation by authorities. Striking the right balance between an innovative market and integrating regulation is a key element of maximizing the values of shared services (Veeneman et al., 2019).

2.4 A user perspective

Eventually, the sharing modes will only make their impact on public transport if travelers want to use them. The impact they are going to make, positive or negative, is highly dependent on how the travelers are going to use them. And how travelers are going to use them is in turn highly dependent on the user experience these shared modes provide (Veeneman et al., 2019).

How users will respond to sharing is still unclear, as many of the choices involved are long-term lifestyle choices. Feigon and Murphy (2016) show that they expect the impact of shared modes to be more substantial on car-ownership than on public transport use, but they still see substitution. With car sharing more frequently used in the off-peak and bike sharing in the peak, they see bike sharing as augmenting public transport and car-sharing and ride-hailing. This is in line with Tirachini and del Río (2019), seeing substitution of public transport by ride hailing, which they link to poor rail quality of services. Nelson and Sadowsky (2019) see an effect of ride-hailing on rail services, but not on bus services in New York. On the other hand, Shaheen and Chan (2016) show reduced use of busses, as some patronage moves to bike sharing. Also, use of rail diminished in big cities. However, in medium sized cities, bike sharing was linked to an increase in public transport patronage. Arendsen (2019) showed how existing travelers using public transport have a relatively high barrier to start using the new shared modes. Travelers often need a pivotal push (they move to a city, extensive road works on their route, they are on holiday) to start traveling differently and use a different mode. However, some shared modes really fit into a particular need in their trip chain. Although this leads to faster adoption, the core of the trip chain is still kept unchanged. For the traveler, the value of shared modes seems highly contextual. It is clear some public transport services will be affected; however, the full impact of these emerging technological developments in transport will only become clear in the rear-view mirror.

For the traveler, integration of mobility services is an important issue, impacting on convenience, wait times and transfer penalties (Ambrosino et al., 2016). As previously stated, more mobility options are filling the gap between public and private transport modes. If travelers want to use those options together, this could lead to rather complicated trip-chains. We see the advent of digital platforms aiming to provide travelers with an 'one App access-all-modes' solution to the finding, reserving, and paying for transport services. These platforms aggregate all the different modes available in a manner that can breakdown the knowledge barrier that would be required to integrate these modes manually. Rather than being loyal to one mode, the platform may suggest a combination of walking, bike share or ride hailing, or public transport, linked to time and cost preferences.

This is where MaaS could come in and play a major role in how the shared modes and public transport will interact. MaaS provides a platform layer over all these different modes of transport. It integrates the different modes for the travelers, providing them with a seamless experience, including the shared modes and public transport (Hirschhorn et al., 2019). Various MaaS functions are already available in the Netherlands. Identification and payment is provided through a national ticketing scheme. Although it is used for public transport travel, bike parking, bike sharing and car sharing, it is still a closed system from within the current operators, which could develop further in the direction of MaaS. We see competing platforms, like MASABI, WHIM, TRANZER and MOOVIT coming from the outside, with growing opportunities as operators open up their sales (Jacobs, 2019).

With various pilots going on in the Netherlands (like in Limburg), first implementations across the globe, like UbiGo in Gothenburg (Smith et al., 2018), the full potential of MaaS as integrator between shared, public and private modes is still largely in development. MaaS implementations could very well tie shared modes, public transport and private modes together for travelers. However, the business case of the additional platform layer could very well be to push the services to the traveler that pay the MaaS platform provider most, distorting travel options.

A key aspect of any integration, including MaaS platforms, is how it optimizes trips for the traveler (see also Veeneman et al., 2018). Most travel planners optimize for least travel time, which is generally in line with the individual optimization of the trip. More collectively oriented optimizations are becoming available: least uncertain arrival time, healthiest, least CO_2, most beautiful, least congested; all possible optimizations that travelers might take into account. Their evaluation of the value of trips could very well change toward more varied evaluations of trips, beyond travel time. This is an important factor in the way in which MaaS can have a real impact in the growth of shared services on public transport through its role toward the traveler. When the MaaS implementations focus on individual gains, the strengths of public transport on a collective level might be overlooked as travelers are pointed elsewhere. If MaaS is implemented in ways that include more collective and public values, public transport could be the mainstay of many trip chains combining public transport and shared modes. How this will develop is still unclear.

Again, there is always the tension between shared modes implemented as competing with or integrating with public transport. Even the implementation of MaaS can be more directed toward either one of these two. A successful MaaS platform can make or break the integration between modes and drive the value of the platform toward its own the business goals, fastest trips for the traveler, or highest values for society. That all depends highly on the way that the platform is implemented (see Hirschhorn et al., 2019).

In addition, the way that platforms are supporting the traveler to integrate different modes of transport could be done in various ways (see also Kamargianni et al., 2016). The above-mentioned MaaS platform could play an important role as the integrator. However, travelers can take a more active role in coordination of their services. Google already provides a level of integrated planning in their Google Maps app.

Authorities can obviously nudge users into using the modes of transport that best support their wider strategic objectives (e.g., emissions and congestion reduction). Anagnostopoulou et al. (2016) show how goal setting, self-monitoring, personalized messaging, social comparisons and gamification can be implemented to drive travelers to collectively use more sustainable modes. Their success in doing so will influence the way in which travelers integrate shared modes in their trip chains and the effect shared modes will have on public transport. Authorities also can focus on the providers of services, which we will discuss below.

2.5 A governance perspective

In most developed countries public transport is highly planned with a great deal of government control. Even in countries like the United Kingdom, where public transport is provided by commercial operators on their own initiative, governments play an important role as they control the infrastructure, provide services like integrated ticketing, provide lowered fares for specific groups, provide a license to operate, etc. The responsibility for different modes is often spread over different levels of government, with lower levels of government responsible for slower, local modes and higher levels of government responsible for faster long-distance modes (Veeneman and Mulley, 2018).

In addition, local authorities also have responsibility for the public space and they often can condition the way in which shared modes are provided in that space. Even when they lack formal powers, we have seen situations were private operators of bike sharing services are choosing to work closely together with local governments (Janmaat, 2019), although the dockless bike share experience in the 2014–18 period was characterized by limited formal coordination between the private operator and government.

This means that governments, on different levels, do play a major role in the way in which the interaction between newly developed shared modes and existing public transport will play out. As previously stated, the implementation of shared modes can be competitive toward public transport or in can be integrative. Only when the business case of the shared mode is positive, the competitive model becomes more likely. But even there we see that governments have instruments that can regulate shared modes. In Singapore, dockless bike share was provided with preferred parking locations, in which an area approximating the size of one or two car parking spaces was demarcated to the parking of share bikes, tied strongly to the existing public transport network (Shen et al., 2018a). In the Netherlands, the Delft and Rotterdam municipality provides designated bike parking areas for the users of bike share services, while the Amsterdam municipality has banned those services outright (Janmaat, 2019), as it struggles to cope with the parking problem caused by large numbers of private bikes parked in a manner that can impinge on street amenity and pedestrian flow.

Hirschhorn et al. (2019) shows how the integration of modes through MaaS is highly dependent on the way that governments see their role. They show how authorities in the Amsterdam area asked operators to provide integration between public transport and shared modes in one concession. The operator included a MaaS platform provider in their bid for the concession, providing a tightly integrated combination, including shared modes. In the Birmingham area, private operators with little control by the local authority asked that authority to bring in a MaaS provider, so the MaaS platform could tie all the different modes together. So, in both countries with high levels of agency over public transport, as well in countries with low agency over public transport, authorities are stepping in to tie the different modes together.

As Veeneman et al. (2019) show, this agency that government have, on different levels, can also be problematic. The innovation in (shared) mobility is coming clearly from the private sector. In terms of governance responses, we see three options. First, to protect existing interest in public transport, authorities could fend off the new shared modes or stifle them to the extent that the added value to the overall system is limited. In this way, the traveler will miss out on the potential innovations the shared services could bring. Second, to allow for the innovation, authorities could provide favorable conditions for shared modes, without much interference into the implementation. In this way, they run the risk of a competitive implementation of the shared modes, eroding the core of public transport and the value it creates and the investments that have been committed. A third option makes the most sense, in which the integration of shared modes and public transport is sought. Shared modes provide great options for those markets for which scheduled and routed public transport services are really ill-equipped and costly. Lines with high levels of demand could be better served with traditional, high capacity public transport, but many niches exist in which the shared modes come to their own.

If efficiently, and with the user experience of the traveler at the center, the third option could create a compelling value proposition to the user and increase the sustainability of the transport system. Instruments that governments have for such a balanced integration are many. Most governments have strong control over infrastructure. They can facilitate shared bike parking at bus stops or in the future, charging stations for autonomous vehicles. They often are responsible for public transport in the form of concessions, where we already have seen attempts to integrate shared modes in traditional public transport concessions. Or even when they have a more limited role in providing public transport, the coordination that they do provide, for example, on integrated ticketing, already proves a basis for moving toward integration.

Tying public transport and shared modes together will create the most value for the traveler, especially when the potential of the shared modes in not stifled by the integration. It could also create the most value for society, as it could capitalize on the value that public transport is already providing and on the investments that already have been made in the sector. In Singapore, this approach is becoming reality (Shen et al., 2018b), with a number of dockless bike share providers. Ambrosino et al. (2016) expect this integration to be highly dependent on the authority. Huwer (2004) also points in that direction. Smith et al. (2018) show the spectrum of shared transport options, from those closely controlled by government, through to environments in which the commercial sector plays the lead role, as well as cities that sit in the middle of these two extremes. Although this is still under development, the role of public agencies, regulating transport in almost all forms and providing public transport services, is still very strong. If they are able to overcome existing administrative and policy hurdles, their role in shaping the success of the integration is not easily overestimated. Public authorities will be the key players in making the link, hopefully without stifling the innovative power of the new shared service providers (see Veeneman et al., 2019).

3. Conclusion and discussion

We are currently in a period of considerable technological innovation that is predicted by many to change the way in which transport is used. As shared mobility platforms proliferate, a world of *access over ownership* is promised, in which travelers are able to select the mode of transport that best suits their immediate needs. The impact this has on public transport is yet to be fully understood, and its impact are unlikely to be known for some time, and will vary from city to city. Moreover, we are said to be on the cusp of the driverless vehicle revolution, turning every Uber, Lyft and Didi into 'robotaxis,' promising to deliver door to door convenience at a fraction of the cost of existing, human driven car services. These technological advances, as well as the many bike share and e-scooter services raises questions as to the degree these new shared mobility services will compete or complement traditional public transport services.

The most extensively used shared mode is the shared bike, which can serve to support public transport use in some contexts, while in others, can be used to replace it (Fishman, 2020; Kager et al., 2016). On the more technological advanced shared modes, like autonomous cars, the expectations are high (Alessandrini et al., 2015), but their effect on mobility as a whole and public transport in particular remains to be seen, as this offering is yet to made on a broad, public scale. If these 'robo-taxis' are offered until the existing pricing structure for car use (i.e., in the absence of a network based road user price based on distance traveled), it is more than plausible that their introduction could erode public transport patronage and increase traffic congestion.

There are a few clear conditioning factors. In an urban context, train and metro are hard to replace. High capacity public transport on congested infrastructure using rail and bus is not easy to supplant with shared modes with a less efficient use of the limited space. Even if a vehicle is shared, that does not make up for the significant space efficiency of public transport (see also Currie, 2018; Walker, 2015). In areas with less dense demand, busses could be supplanted by shared modes. That is already happening and seems promising in those cases where bus services are simply too costly for the level of demand. In the cases discussed here, public authorities are driving these changes and integrate the new forms with existing public transport. In that case, the relation between shared modes and public transport can be synergetic.

Fully coordinated autonomous vehicles might improve the performance of shared modes in terms of spatial efficiency, but there is a very long way to go before the majority of vehicles in the fleet will have autonomous capabilities, and even when they do, their ability to navigate urban streets is under question. For city governments seeking to ensure their transport system aligns with their wider strategic objectives, it is likely to be necessary for the introduction of regulation, and this may include mechanisms to encourage a complementary relationship with tradition, high capacity public transport services.

The big challenge will be to balance governmental roles, driving the new services away from competition with public transport and toward integration. This should be done in a way that keeps the incentive to innovate alive in the private sector and provides travelers with attractive new forms of an integrated system of transport.

References

Alessandrini, A., Campagna, A., Delle Site, P., Filippi, F., Persia, L., 2015. Automated vehicles and the rethinking of mobility and cities. Transp. Res. Procedia 5, 145–160.

Ambrosino, G., Nelson, J.D., Boero, M., Pettinelli, I., 2016. Enabling intermodal urban transport through complementary services: from flexible mobility services to the shared use mobility agency: workshop 4. Developing inter-modal transport systems. Res. Transp. Econ. 59, 179–184.

Anagnostopoulou, E., Bothos, E., Magoutas, B., Schrammel, J., Mentzas, G., 2016. Persuasive Technologies for Sustainable Urban Mobility, 1-11. arXiv. preprint arXiv:1604.05957. https://pdfs.semanticscholar.org/3c06/88b9e34091f52f6d896fd624e8db7b08ae0c.pdf.

Arendsen, J., 2019. Shared Mobility for the First and Last Mile: Exploring the Willingness to Share. Delft University of Technology, Delft.

Bakker, S., 2018. Electric two-wheelers, sustainable mobility and the city. In: Sustainable Cities-Authenticity, Ambition and Dream. IntechOpen, Chicago.

Banister, D., 2008. The sustainable mobility paradigm. Transp. Policy 15 (2), 73–80.

Boor, S., 2019. Impact of 4th Generation Bike Sharing; a Case Study of Delft. Delft University of Technology, Delft.

CBS, 2016. Transport en Mobiliteit (in Dutch). CBS, Den Haag.

Cervero, R., 2017. Mobility niches: jitneys to robo-taxis. J. Am. Plann. Assoc. 83 (4), 404–412.

CROW, 2015. Kostenkengetallen regionaal openbaar vervoer (in Dutch). CROW, Utrecht.

Currie, G., 2018. Lies, damned lies, AVs, shared mobility, and urban transit futures. J. Public Transp. 21 (1), 3.

Fagnant, D.J., Kockelman, K., 2015. Preparing a nation for autonomous vehicles: opportunities, barriers and policy recommendations. Transp. Res. A Policy Pract. 77, 167–181.

Feigon, S., Murphy, C., 2016. TCRP Report 188: Shared Mobility and the Transformation of Public Transit. Transportation Research Board of the National Academies, Washington, DC.

Fishman, E., 2016. Bikeshare: a review of recent literature. Transplant. Rev. 36 (1), 92–113.

Fishman, E., 2020. Bike Share. Routledge, New York. ISBN-13: 978-1138682498.

Hirschhorn, F., Veeneman, W., van de Velde, D., 2018. Inventory and rating of performance indicators and organisational features in metropolitan public transport: A worldwide Delphi survey. Res. Transp. Econ. 69, 144–156.

Hirschhorn, F., Paulsson, A., Sørensen, C.H., Veeneman, W., 2019. Public transport regimes and mobility as a service: Governance approaches in Amsterdam, Birmingham, and Helsinki. Transp. Res. A Policy Pract. 130, 178–191.

Hudson, M., Levy, C., Nicholson, J., Macrory, R., Snelson, P., 1982. Bicycle Planning: Policy and Practice. No. Monograph, Architectural Press.

Huwer, U., 2004. Public transport and csar-sharing—benefits and effects of combined services. Transp. Policy 11 (1), 77–87.

Jacobs, I., 2019. Doel MaaS-Platform Past bij onze Taak als Publieke Vervoerders. OV Pro. https://www.ovpro.nl/special/2019/05/28/doel-maas-platform-past-bij-onze-taak-als-publieke-vervoerders. visited September 15th 2019.

Janmaat, Y., 2019. The Governance of Dockless Bicycle Sharing Delft. Delft University of Technology.

Kager, R., Bertolini, L., Te Brömmelstroet, M., 2016. Characterisation of and reflections on the synergy of bicycles and public transport. Transp. Res. A Policy Pract. 85, 208–219.

Kamargianni, M., Li, W., Matyas, M., Schäfer, A., 2016. A critical review of new mobility services for urban transport. Transp. Res. Procedia 14, 3294–3303.

KIM (2018) Mobiliteitsbeeld 2016, http://web.minienm.nl/mob2016/1_8.html; visited August 20th 2019

Li, Z., Hong, Y., Zhang, Z., 2016. An empirical analysis of on-demand ride sharing and traffic congestion. In: Proceedings of the International Conference on Information Systems.

Litman, T., 2000. Evaluating carsharing benefits. Transp. Res. Rec. 1702 (1), 31–35.
Muñoz, J.C., Gschwender, A., 2008. Transantiago: a tale of two cities. Res. Transp. Econ. 22 (1), 45–53.
Nelson, E., Sadowsky, N., 2019. Estimating the impact of ride-hailing app company entry on public transportation use in major US urban areas. The BE J. Econ. Anal. Policy 19 (1).
Noel, E.C., 1988. Park-and-ride: alive, well, and expanding in the United States. J. Urban Plann. Dev. 114 (1), 2–13.
Parkhurst, G., 2000. Influence of bus-based park and ride facilities on users' car traffic. Transp. Policy 7 (2), 159–172.
Parkinson, T., Fisher, I., 1996. TCRP report 13: rail transit capacity. TRB. National Research Council, Washington, D.C.
Shaheen, S., Chan, N., 2016. Mobility and the sharing economy: potential to facilitate the first-and last-mile public transit connections. Built Environ. 42 (4), 573–588.
Shen, Y., Zhang, H., Zhao, J., 2018a. Integrating shared autonomous vehicle in public transportation system: a supply-side simulation of the first-mile service in Singapore. Transp. Res. A Policy Pract. 113, 125–136.
Shen, Y., Zhang, X., Zhao, J., 2018b. Understanding the usage of dockless bike sharing in Singapore. Int. J. Sustain. Transp. 12.9 (2018), 686–700.
Smith, G., Sochor, J., Karlsson, I.M., 2018. Mobility as a service: development scenarios and implications for public transport. Res. Transp. Econ. 69, 592–599.
Standing, C., Standing, S., Biermann, S., 2019. The implications of the sharing economy for transport. Transp. Rev. 39 (2), 226–242.
Tirachini, A., del Río, M., 2019. Ride-hailing in Santiago de Chile: users' characterisation and effects on travel behaviour. Transp. Policy 82, 46–57.
van Nes, R., Hamerslag, R., Immers, L.H., 1988. The Design of Public Transport Networks. National Research Council, Transportation Research Board, p. vol. 1202.
Veeneman, W., Mulley, C., 2018. Multi-level governance in public transport: governmental layering and its influence on public transport service solutions. Res. Transp. Econ. 69, 430–437.
Veeneman, W., van der Voort, H., Hirschhorn, F., Steenhuisen, B., Klievink, B., 2018. PETRA: governance as a key success factor for big data solutions in mobility. Res. Transp. Econ. 69, 420–429.
Veeneman, W., Van Kuijk, J.I., Hiemstra-van Mastrigt, S., 2019. Dreaming of the travellers experience in 2040: exploring governance strategies and their consequences for personal mobility systems. In: Mueler, B., Meyer, G. (Eds.), Towards User Centric Transport. Springer.
Vuchic, V.R., 2017. Urban Transit: Operations, Planning, and Economics. John Wiley & Sons.
Walker, J., 2015. Self Driving Cars a Coming Congestion Disaster. https://humantransit.org/2015/11/self-driving-cars-a-coming-congestion-disaster.html. visited August 20th 2019.
Walters, J., 2008. Overview of public transport policy developments in South Africa. Res. Transp. Econ. 22 (1), 98–108.
Wang, M., Zhou, X., 2017. Bike-sharing systems and congestion: evidence from US cities. J. Transp. Geogr. 65, 147–154.
Wirtz, J., Tang, C., 2016. Uber: competing as market leader in the US versus being a distant second in China. Serv. Mark. 626–632.

Further reading

Alonso-González, M.J., van Oort, N., Oded, C., Hoogendoorn, S., 2017. Urban demand responsive transport in the mobility as a service ecosystem: its role and potential market share. In: Conference on Competition and Ownership in Land Passenger Transport, Stockholm.

CHAPTER FOUR

Sharing vehicles and sharing rides in real-time: Opportunities for self-driving fleets

Krishna Murthy Gurumurthy[a], Kara M. Kockelman[a,]*, Benjamin J. Loeb[b]

[a]Department of Civil, Architectural and Environmental Engineering, The University of Texas at Austin, Austin, TX, United States
[b]Delaware Valley Regional Planning Commission, Philadelphia, PA, United States
*Corresponding author: e-mail address: kkockelm@mail.utexas.edu

Contents

Abstract

Access to shared and fully-automated or 'autonomous' vehicles (SAVs) is coming, and expected to be popular and cost-effective, especially for city dwellers. This chapter synthesizes and summarizes research on SAVs, including dynamic ride-sharing (en route), range-constrained electric SAV (SAEV) operations, SAV fleet costs, and variable road pricing in a world of AVs, where vehicle-miles traveled (VMT) rise and congestion worsens. Researchers consistently find that a single SAV with long range and fast refueling can replace six or more household vehicles in countries with high vehicle ownership, even when serving long-distance trips. That number falls a bit when SAVs are range constrained and/or have long recharging times. Zero-occupancy VMT, called empty VMT, will be a problem for urban-network congestion levels if travelers do not share rides with strangers (increasing average vehicle occupancy) and road tolls are not included. Expected costs are consistently under USD $0.75 per revenue-mile, assuming the self-driving technology adds USD $25,000 or less to each conventional vehicle.

Advances in Transport Policy and Planning, Volume 4
ISSN 2543-0009
https://doi.org/10.1016/bs.atpp.2019.09.001

SAEVs will bring some emission savings when vehicle-to-grid consumption is managed well. Fleet sizing, fare economics and regional policies will be key to managing this SAV future.

Keywords: Shared mobility, Autonomous, Shared autonomous vehicles, Dynamic ride-sharing, Electric vehicles, Future transport, Pricing

Abbreviation

aBus	autonomous bus
AV	autonomous vehicle
AVO	average vehicle occupancy
DRS	dynamic ride-sharing
DTA	dynamic traffic assignment
EV	electric vehicle
ICE	internal combustion engine
MATSim	multi-agent transport simulation
O-D	origin-destination
OEM	original equipment manufacturer
SAEV	shared autonomous electric vehicle
SAV	shared autonomous vehicle
TNC	transportation network company
V2G	vehicle-to-grid
VMT	vehicle-miles traveled
WTP	willingness to pay

1. Background

Fully-automated or autonomous vehicles (AVs), referred to as Level 4 AVs according to SAE International,[a] are in an advanced testing phase in the U.S. states of Arizona, California, Pennsylvania, and Texas, among others. It will be no surprise if AVs are widely available for public use in the next 5 years. Technology companies, like Waymo (AV subsidiary of Alphabet Inc.) and Uber (Transportation Network Company, or TNC), are spearheading innovation in AV technology alongside original equipment manufacturers (OEMs), and significant progress has been made in as little as the last decade. Boasting benefits in several realms, such as travel time, energy

[a] SAE demarcates 5 levels of autonomy, with level 4 and 5 being fully-autonomous and the other lower levels needing human input. Level 5 differs from 4 in the AVs ability to drive off-road and without connectivity or feedback from the infrastructure (https://saemobilus.sae.org/content/j3016_201609).

and safety, AVs are geared to disrupt the market in the next decade (Kockelman et al., 2016, 2018). The benefits they have to offer, however, do come with a high price-tag. As in any industry, the cost of innovation is eventually burdened on the consumer, and, consequently, AVs are expected to be expensive to own, at least in the early stages of deployment. This chapter focuses on a particular near-term, and potential long-term, alternative to AV ownership: shared AVs (SAVs).

A fleet of SAVs operated by one entity and shared by a community can be used to make trips and operate with minimal human intervention. One central control-unit will likely be sufficient to perform all operations for the entire fleet, thereby significantly cutting down the required human capital. SAVs are also expected to be more profitable than current forms of car-sharing and ride-hailing services, largely owing to the absence of driver-related costs and human error (Fagnant and Kockelman, 2015). The improved safety of AVs will also mean that operators may pay lower insurance premiums, and this will allow them the flexibility to charge lower fares while having a similar or better profit margin as compared to today's ride-hailing services (Clements and Kockelman, 2017). Aside from the profitability of the fleet from an operator's perspective, they will also provide a convenient yet affordable, door-to-door service for everyone. Nowadays, people tend to use their personal vehicles inefficiently, i.e., with several empty seats and for only about 1 h a day, on average (Fagnant and Kockelman, 2018). Personal vehicles may be the most convenient alternative now, but they may start to seem expensive in contrast to SAVs. When they begin to make better use of these unused seats via dynamic ride-sharing (or DRS, where strangers share rides for a part of their trip), SAVs can keep fares to a minimum. Shared usage, especially in conjunction with cleaner technology like electric propulsion, can produce impressive environmental benefits (Farhan and Chen, 2018).

Shared mobility is an obvious next step to utilizing AVs efficiently and research on this topic is in its infancy. This chapter aims to review the different dimensions of studies previously completed on this topic and provides an anticipated trajectory for future research. Some of the key elements covered here are the operational aspects of SAV use, travel demand for shared mobility, costs of these services, impact of electrification, and policies to better accommodate this evolving option.

Research on SAVs has been a hot topic for less than a decade, but numerous researchers from around the globe have generated many valuable articles on different facets of SAV use. Consistent with nomenclature used in this chapter, most researchers use the term 'SAV' for 4-seater vehicles, and 'aBuses' for larger-capacity shared autonomous vehicles. Terms like 'autonomous mobility-on-demand' (AMoD), 'shared use automated mobility services' (SAMS), and 'autonomous Taxis' (ATs or aTaxis) are also used. The following sections detail different dimensions of SAV and aBus research, ending with descriptions of literature gaps worthy of further exploration.

2. From sharing vehicles to sharing rides

ZipCar began its operation in early 2000 and was key in popularizing car-sharing. The growing popularity of AVs due to the DARPA challenge (Buehler et al., 2009) encouraged several researchers to delve into a mixture of AVs and car-sharing. Burns et al. (2013) used aggregated trip data for three U.S. regions (Ann Arbor, Michigan; Babcock Ranch, Florida; and Manhattan, New York) to solve, both analytically (using pre-defined relationship to system metrics) and using simulation, for an approximate fleet requirement. Their results suggested that 2,000–18,000 SAVs were required depending on the region's trip density and total number of trips in peak periods. Fleet utilization varied between 70% and 90% in peak periods and had reasonable response times. Although their research made significant assumptions (like uniform origin-destination [O-D] distribution) to simplify the process of estimation, it was one of the first studies on SAVs, quantifying metrics like empty driving and customer wait times. Some of these shortcomings were addressed by Spieser et al. (2014) in their study for Singapore using a more robust methodology. Using real trip data from a travel survey fused with network statistics from a taxi dataset, they showed that Singapore's travel demand could be satisfied with a shared fleet just one-third the size of of the then existing vehicle fleet. Both these studies strongly recommended the transition to SAVs, but also advised caution on the increase in vehicle-miles traveled (VMT) that can result from unoccupied travel. Fagnant and Kockelman (2014) were able to quantify this rise in VMT at 11% from studying travel patterns on a grid representing downtown Austin, Texas. A higher replacement rate of 11–1 (i.e., the number of conventional vehicles that can be replaced by one SAV) was observed in this study, which is nearly four times as much as determined by Spieser et al.

Brownell and Kornhauser (2014) explored the use of SAVs at a much larger scale. Travel behavior for the entire state of New Jersey was aggregated in grids, arising from satellite feed pixels, due to the lack of a detailed road network. Their analysis tested SAVs as a paratransit service, and primarily showed that allowing O-D aggregation for pickup and drop off (rather than fixed stops) increased average vehicle occupancy (AVO), i.e., number of travelers accommodated in one vehicle, due to increased convenience and comfort from closer pickup and drop off points. Similar to Spieser et al. (2014), the entire state's travel demand could be served by one-third the size of the personally-owned fleet, but it is important to note that Brownell and Kornhauser (2014) simulated a preliminary version of DRS. Burghout et al. (2015) were able to use a detailed network for Stockholm, Sweden but with a limitation of only zone level O-D available for personal vehicle trips. They were able to test three subsets of DRS matched at the zone level, i.e., trips with common O-D pairs, trips with common O's but different D's, and trips with different O's but common D's. Owing to zone level information, intra-zonal travel time was assumed, and travel times were fixed at a fraction of the free-flow speed. An overall reduction in VMT was observed, thanks to DRS, with a fleet just 5% the size of the private fleet serving all trips. Although a version of DRS was tested by Brownell and Kornhauser (2014) and Burghout et al. (2015), severe aggregation and use of static travel times may have led to optimistic results of AVO and replacement rate (in hindsight) for the scenarios tested. It was common consensus that a simulation-based analysis using dynamic traffic assignment (DTA), was required to understand the impact of an SAV fleet, and especially that of DRS.

2.1 Large-scale agent-based simulations

Simulation-based studies tried to incorporate realistic behavior but realism was added step- by- step over time, beginning with the goal of understanding an SAV fleet's operation without DRS. The increased need for realism in travel demand modeling, in terms of both spatial and temporal scales, resulted in the development of an agent-based model called the Multi-Agent Transport Simulation, or MATSim (Horni et al., 2016), and it quickly became popular for its ability to run transport simulations on a large scale. Fagnant et al. (2015) simulated SAVs on an idealized grid-network, of longitudinal and lateral links of equal length, representing downtown Austin, Texas, and using hour-by-hour travel times from MATSim. A sample of trips from the region's travel demand model was simulated to use SAVs to account for uncertainty of the initial market toward AVs, while also spatially constraining the SAV operation to the downtown area. Their 24-h weekday simulation found that each SAV could make all the trips originally made by nine conventional vehicles, and this was much higher than the replacement rate of 3 to 1 found in Spieser et al. but much lower than the 20 to 1 estimated by Burghout et al. This was extraordinary considering that Austin's population was only one-fifth that of Singapore in 2015, and, therefore, Austin likely had a much lower trip density. The discrepancy may also have stemmed from their downtown study area, as opposed to Spieser et al.'s study of an entire region. However, Fagnant et al. also found an estimated 8% increase in VMT from SAVs operating unoccupied. On the bright side, their results did show better utilization of the fleet, and, therefore, possibility of reduced emissions from fewer cold starts and faster turnover of the fleet. Bösch et al. (2016) also conducted a similar analysis, using demand generated for Zurich, Switzerland in MATSim, running SAV simulations outside the MATSim environment. Their results of a 10 to 1 vehicle replacement ratio validated Fagnant et al. high rate, even when assuming 10% market penetration. From their 1,000 scenarios simulated, they were able to show that required fleet size was a function of coverage area rather than the demand served. In both these MATSim-related simulations, the main limitation was that SAVs were not simulated internally with congestion feedback.

Taking the next step in SAV simulations, Bischoff and Maciejewski (2016) integrated a dynamically-responsive SAV fleet within MATSim to observe congestion effects. Their work simulated 100,000 SAVs for Berlin, serving 2.5 million trips, and observed a 10–1 replacement rate for conventional vehicles, thus supporting the simplifications made by Fagnant et al. and Bösch et al. (2016). Results from their simulation showed increase in drive time (up to 17%) as compared to before the SAV service, which can be a proxy for VMT increase as observed by Fagnant et al., but no significant delays were seen. Although absence of significant congestion was attributed to better flow by SAVs potentially coordinating on the roadway, this is unlikely in the near-term because of safety concerns and human drivers fearing tight headways to SAVs, at least initially.

2.2 Simulating dynamic ride-sharing

An increase in VMT was a common conclusion in the literature at this point which would eventually lead to increased congestion, despite several personally-owned vehicles being replaced. With prior research supporting the benefits of DRS, albeit with limitations, a natural next step was to observe network-wide impacts when an SAV service is operated with DRS. Fagnant et al.'s (2015) model on the gridded-network for Austin,

Texas was extended by Fagnant and Kockelman (2018) to include DRS capabilities. Several conditions for added travel time to riders were included to filter away unrealistic ride-matching (with travelers experiencing high wait times or added delays) and an overall increase in the SAV fleet's serviceability was observed. This study, which was published 2016, showed that the 8% increase in VMT that was previously observed, was at least partially mitigated, even with only a sample of the population using DRS. Adding more flexibility to the ride-matching procedure (like allowing greater than a 40% increase in travel time from DRS as opposed to direct O-D travel time, but with wait time constrained to approximately 10 min) capped rising VMT at 1%. When more travelers (11% of the region's demand) where simulated to use the service, the overall VMT decreased. DRS was, therefore, seen as a potential solution to the rising congestion.

Maciejewski et al. (2017) documented ride-matching and traffic flow related algorithms used by Bischoff and Maciejewski, and introduced modifications to MATSim (specifically, by programmatically solving the dynamic vehicle routing problem) that allowed them to simulate DRS. This was further enhanced by Hörl (2017) when he tested how an SAV fleet behaved when rides were shared compared to when they were not. By simulating a fleet where half the vehicles explicitly offered DRS at a discount and the other half offered a personal ride, Hörl was able to show that DRS may be preferred at off-peaks. This is due to the discounted cost of a shared ride, together with low off-peak demand that reduced chances of matching, and consequently, added delay. Personal rides were preferred during the peak to benefit from the absence of added delay. Using the popular Sioux Falls test network, Hörl also simulated the fleet twice, once offering DRS and once offering only personal rides, to discuss efficient seat usage and attained a 1.64 maximum AVO with DRS, but was unable to comment on VMT because of the artificial network used. Better utilization of empty seats may be seen as a proxy for curbing rising VMT, but route deviations arising from DRS may have outweighed the saved VMT.

Around the same time, Levin et al. (2017) developed a similar DRS application in a simulator that incorporated more realistic traffic flow for their case study of Austin, Texas. Their study provided a more measured assessment of AVs benefits using realistic flow models, as opposed to more optimistic results from past studies that did not take into account congestion effects. Shorter travel times and reduction in VMT was observed only when a small fleet of around 2,000 SAVs with DRS served nearly 63,000 trips in

Austin's CBD for 2 h in the AM peak. Increasing fleet size decreased the necessity to share rides and decreased fleet utilization (i.e., many SAVs were idle). Each SAV was serving, on average, 31 trips in 1 day (each trip averaging 2.3 mi), which is comparable to that observed by Fagnant and Kockelman (2018) in their simulation with 11% of the region's demand.

Martinez and Viegas (2017) studied a fleet of SAVs operating in Lisbon, Portugal, and included mode choice in their simulation. Two types of shared vehicles were available to choose from: 4-seater AVs and either 8- or 16-seater aBus, in addition to walk, or subway as available modes with the choice made based on an estimated model (substituting taxi and buses for their AV alternative). As a first in the literature, overall VMT was reduced by an astonishing 30% in their study when SAVs and aBuses were available, with results indicating significant emission benefits as well. A large AVO of 2.0 in SAVs and 4.2 in aBuses is likely the most significant contributor to this large decrease in VMT. This combined fleet of SAVs and aBuses could replace nearly 10 conventional vehicles per automated vehicle.

Another study to include mode choice was Liu et al. (2017) who also studied SAV fare impacts, but without DRS. They modeled choice between conventional vehicles, transit and SAVs, and served SAV requests with a wait time threshold of 10 min. Although they observed significant energy and emission savings by considering better drive cycles for AVs (Kockelman and Boyles, 2018), the increase in VMT from the absence of DRS, and resulting congestion, was found at all fare levels. Further, the authors highlighted the importance of modeling destination choices for future studies to capture changes in trip distribution while using low-cost SAVs. Heilig et al. (2017) solved this problem with a case study for Stuttgart, Germany. Their model allowed choices for walking, biking, transit and sharing rides in SAVs, along with destination choice. They found overall VMT in Stuttgart reduced by about 20% using a relatively small fleet, just 15% the size of the existing private vehicle fleet, but similar to Bösch et al. (2016), they did not simulate DRS. Interestingly, the walk, bike and transit modal shares in Liu et al. future scenario increased, similar to Heilig et al. (2017), although one might assume that low-cost alternatives of 50 ¢/mile for SAVs would prevent this. Zhao and Kockelman (2018), used a more familiar approach of a four-step demand model, and tested fare sensitivities when destination choice was modeled. Spanning nine scenarios, they showed that VMT increased under different operating costs, parking costs, and tolls.

2.3 Operational nuances, parking and solving the first-mile-last-mile problem

The SAV literature's focus eventually shifted from direct applications of SAV and DRS operations to understanding more nuanced information relating to concepts like proactive vehicle relocations and ride-matching processes, as noted next, as well as parking demand changes and first-mile-last-mile (FMLM) benefits.

An SAV fleet's operational efficiency and ride-matching rate were tested by Hörl et al. (2018) and Ruch et al. (2018) using a common framework. The studies focused on testing two ride-matching algorithms (a simple heuristics and a bipartite optimization routine) and two rebalancing techniques for case studies of Zurich and San Francisco using MATSim's traffic assignment module. Their results suggested that smart matching and rebalancing algorithms are able to quickly match travelers to their SAVs, and can give an advantage in the market when several companies are competing for demand. However, from a single operator perspective, reduction in wait times proved to be beneficial. Hyland and Mahmassani (2018) tested six distinct dispatch strategies for an SAV fleet without DRS simulated using the Manhattan, New York grid. Their study revealed that fleet size and empty VMT depend on the spatial structure (e.g., dense or sprawling) of the region, and that these metrics are improved for any future SAV fleet using an optimized dispatch strategy. Their research helps inform initial SAV operators dispatch strategies based on the region and their objective.

Large availability of travel data from cellphone records, prompted Gurumurthy and Kockelman (2018) to conduct a benchmark test for DRS. Their study, based on travel in Orlando, Florida, generated the region's demand and simulated them as served by an SAV fleet with DRS. The initial aggregate dataset was discretized temporally and spatially and DRS-based data analytics showed that around 60% of single-occupant trips in the region could be served by 60,000 SAVs, or 25 person-trips per vehicle. This is lower than the 31 person-trips served per SAV in Fagnant and Kockelman (2018) but the discrepancy arose mainly from the sprawling region and special nature of recreational trips in Orlando. This study validated Hyland and Mahmassani's (2018) hypothesis on spatial structure with around 3% added VMT when ride-matches were maximized. However, it is important to note that even under sprawling conditions, DRS was found to be viable.

SAVs are expected to lower parking demands, at least in downtown areas and other big trip attractors (like airports and hospitals). However, very few studies have analyzed parking demand changes. Using a simple simulation model, Zhang et al. (2015) predicted an optimistic 90% decrease in parking demand on a 10-mile hypothetical grid with only 2% of the population using SAVs, and even greater parking demand reductions based on the willingness to share rides. 2 years later, using a model that allowed discrete-time-based simulations, Zhang and Guhathakurta (2017) estimate 5% less parking land required across Atlanta, thanks to just 5% of vehicle owners shifting to SAVs. Moreover, parking demand was estimated to shift away from downtown spaces to low-income areas if parking charges are assessed and privately owned AVs are allowed to drive empty in search of lower-cost parking. More recently, Millard-Ball (2019) focused on parking demand using travel data from the San Francisco demand models and tested how parking behavior affected the system by comparing parking as before, free-for-all parking, SAVs returning home, and SAVs cruising around. He concludes that a shift to SAVs would not be beneficial overall, due to more driving and added congestion, and recommends using a time-based charge for SAV usage, irrespective of whether it is parked or moving. In a region's CBD, this may be useful to apply across the board.

Shared AVs with DRS, self-driving minibuses, and other versions of aBuses can also serve travelers in lieu of existing buses, in addition to delivering travelers to and from train stations, much like present-day TNCs offering a lower cost ride-sharing alternative. Liang et al. (2016) considered SAV service for a train station in Delft, Netherlands. FMLM service was designed using profit-maximization strategies that served all requests. This zone level study concluded that the FMLM service can be profitable, though this study used fixed demand. Average VMT increased per vehicle with small fleet sizes, but no comment was made on network impacts. Scheltes and de Almeida Correia (2017) extended that work, to analyze network metrics via simulations that reflect additional SAV nuances (like dispatch and relocation) and test the impact of an SAV's travel speed. Relocation strategies increased response times, but even with FMLM, increased overall VMT and added congestion. Shen et al. (2018) included DRS in their FMLM study and focused on when and where SAVs can best complement existing transit lines. They conclude that replacing underutilized bus lines or other forms of transit with SAVs will be beneficial. Farhan et al. (2018) sought to optimize SAV operations via DRS and were able to achieve a VMT reduction of nearly 37%, vs without using DRS in Seattle. de Pinto et al. (2018) used a dynamic assignment model to incorporate many details of transit use, such as boarding and alighting times and queue formation based on available space within transit vehicles. They analyzed how FMLM-serving SAVs can benefit transit systems, and found that SAV fares vs transit fares impacted mode choice significantly. Their bi-level solution framework showed that, overall, SAVs are expected to be a viable option for FMLM use (especially with DRS), in terms of network benefits.

3. Energy and emissions

Utilizing the SAV fleet better than existing personal vehicle fleet will lead to some emission improvements. Fagnant and Kockelman (2014) showed that reduction in cold and warm starts (to 0.05 and 0.7, respectively, per person trip) from shifting to an SAV fleet can reduce CO_2 emissions and particulate matter in the air. These results stayed true even with a better simulation framework by Fagnant et al. (2015) showing an 85% reduction in cold starts. SAVs and aBuses offering DRS as in Martinez and Viegas (2017) were able to reduce CO_2 emissions by almost 40% across all road modes.

Electrification can mitigate some of the issues caused by SAVs with internal combustion engines. These include eliminating engine idling, lower emissions to counteract added VMT and a quieter experience for the customer. EVs are also well suited for the ultra-rigorous use of an SAV fleet with likely less maintenance needs without the complexity of an ICE powertrain. The idea of electrified SAVs (or SAEVs) has gained the interest of researchers lately with many conducting agent-based models to understand how these systems operate. Researchers' goal is generally to determine the feasibility of electrifying an SAV fleet, so the first step is looking at system performance. Gasoline vehicles' nearly immediate refuel times and ubiquitous refueling stations make range a non-issue, but for EVs, recouping range can be a concern. In the near future, cities may have the power grid and charging infrastructure needed to provide inconsequential charge times, but in the meantime it is not obvious if SAEVs can deliver timely, on-demand transportation service with today's technology. Chen et al. (2016), Kang et al. (2016), Yang et al. (2017) and Loeb et al. (2018), all simulate SAEV fleets, focusing on response times and necessary fleet sizes. These papers published between 2016 and 2018 have modeled SAEV fleets with increasing complexity.

Chen et al. (2016) modeled SAEVs in a generic grid imitating a large, metropolitan area with a dense, urban core. Trips were generated at a rate based on their proximity to the center of the area. The fleet and charging stations were generated based on demand through a 'warm start' period to encourage reasonable vehicle start locations and charging station placement. Their goals were to understand how charge time and vehicle range affected the fleet size and the number of charging stations needed to serve demand quickly. They found a fleet of 200-mile range vehicles could be 20% smaller than one composed of vehicles with 80-mile range and 30-min fast-charging reduced fleet size by 30% compared to 4-h charge times. Combining fast-charging and long range gave a 44% decrease in fleet compared to lower ranges and slower charging. The number of charging stations needed to meet demand did not vary much based on these modeling settings, but the number of chargers at each station could be cut by 45% when upgrading from slow charging to fast-charging for the short range case and cut by 86% for the long range case. Vehicle response times for trip requests was 7–10 min on average, unoccupied travel accounted for 10–14% of SAEV VMT (a very small portion of which was for charging) and each vehicle could replace up to 6.8 privately owned vehicles based on daily trip-making rates.

Yang et al. (2017) used a more specific and detailed simulation environment modeled after Shanghai China. They collected a month's worth of taxi travel behavior data from 13,761 vehicles, over 23% of Shanghai's taxi fleet. This was used to map Shanghai into a grid, and trips were generated in each tile according to collected data (similar to methods used by Brownell and Kornhauser, 2014). Vehicles in the simulation environment were dispatched in an unusual first-come, last-served system, where vehicles that ended a trip most recently were dispatched first. This was in order to reduce vehicle idle time. Several vehicle ranges were tested, varying from 93 to 217 miles. 73% of vehicles were able to conduct a full day's taxi operations without charging when equipped with 217-mile range. Full-load ratio (the ratio of occupied VMT to total VMT) was 89% in the simulation compared to 67% in (non-autonomous) observed data. They calculated that the SAEVs could reduce the total taxi fleet size by 41%, but each SAEV idled for an average of 15 h a day, which means the replacement rate could likely be higher.

Kang et al. (2016) took a slightly different approach by modeling an autonomous car-sharing service, where vehicles perform charging trips and meet passengers autonomously, but are human-driven when occupied by a user so as to more seamlessly emulate the experience of a traditional car-sharing service. Rather than simply borrow trip data from literature, Kang et al. estimated demand through an iterative process with a profit-maximizing objective. Their model is an in an 11 × 11 mile square simulating Ann Arbor, Michigan. Similar to Chen et al. findings, they determined that metrics like wait time are not effected by vehicle range and charge times so long as the vehicle fleet is sufficiently large. Charging stations were placed throughout the region at locations which minimize the average distance needed to travel to them. They assumed 30 min were needed to charge a 24 kWh (80-mile) battery to 80%. They found reasonable wait times of 11.9 min, a bit slower than 9.7 min for a non-electrified fleet.

Farhan and Chen (2018) incorporated DRS into Chen et al. (2016)'s model with an optimization framework to obtain best matches. Their results showed that fleet sizes could be further decreased with DRS, and DRS was effective even when vehicles fit only two travelers. The number of charging stations required also decreased with a net increase in benefits, but a drop in VMT was not confirmed.

Loeb et al. (2018), inspired by Chen et al. (2016), used a detailed SAEV simulation environment, modeling the Austin, Texas region using a true network and zonal data as supplied by the local metropolitan planning organization. Trips on the network were modeled with state-of-the-art activity based modeling and dynamic traffic assignment in MATSim. Many concepts were borrowed from Chen et al., such as generating charging stations based on trip demand and testing a series of charging speeds and vehicle ranges. Unlike Chen et al. (2016); however, fleet sizes were fixed for each scenario and many more scenarios were tested. They found that response time was heavily dependent on charging speeds, going from under 4 min at 30-min charge times to over 9 min with 4-h charge. Vehicle range did not have nearly the same impact on response times, except with 4-h charging time which forced response time from 9 min at 93-mile range to 35 min at 62-mile range (electric range that was fairly typical at the time but would not be acceptable in today's new EV market). Fleet size was by far the most impactful for response time. A fleet size equivalent to nine travelers per vehicle gave response times of nearly 25 min with 30-min charge times and 62-mile range. Increasing the fleet size to just seven travelers per vehicle dropped response times to under 8 min for the same range and charge time. For all scenarios, unoccupied VMT hovered around 20% of all VMT.

Liu et al. (2018) used Ann Arbor's travel demand model to quantify the energy use with SAVs and SAEVs, showing that both these fleets did not significantly help with curbing energy use or emissions compared to present-day vehicle fleets. There was an overall increase in energy use from empty VMT, and switching to electric propulsion increased SO_2 emissions (a toxic pollutant) due to the emission intensity observed in Michigan's electric-grid. However, the overall energy use decreased for SAEVs as compared to gasoline-powered SAVs. Another study by Lee and Kockelman (2019) used results from some of prior simulation studies mentioned here (Loeb et al., 2018; Loeb and Kockelman, 2019) and supported the positive effect that SAEVs will have in terms of energy and emissions reduction. Even though these vehicles will need to add charging trips to their itinerary, their research show that, overall, even with pessimistic estimates, the energy use was lower and emission reduction was higher when a fleet of SAEVs are used compared to non-electrified vehicles.

4. Enabling real-time road pricing

Futuristic AV technology enables much more than a profitable operation of a fleet of SAVs. State of the art automation along with high-speed connectivity offered by 5G technology will enable better targeting of our current-day road pricing techniques. As one may anticipate, this will be especially beneficial in the near future in aiding several local and federal authorities who are trying to mitigate rising congestion. Advanced real-time road pricing applied along with SAVs can hold many benefits.

Sharon et al. (2017) first studied one such advanced policy which they termed delta-tolling. The idea behind the technique is to use measures such as current travel time and free-flow travel time, (easily obtainable using advanced 5G technology), to calculate appropriate tolls such that congestion reduces and the overall social welfare of the system increases. The authors did not particularly test a system of SAVs, but this study forms a backbone for futuristic pricing policies that are tested in other studies noted below.

The first study to jointly analyze SAVs and advanced pricing policies was Simoni et al. (2019). The authors compared several pricing policies in two futuristic settings: one where privately owned AVs dominate, and the other where SAVs dominate. Their results set the precedent to overcome increasing VMT from single-occupant SAVs, in a world where travelers are rather unwilling to share in the near future. Two congestion pricing schemes were tested: marginal cost pricing and a travel- time-based congestion pricing. Marginal cost pricing assesses the optimal toll depending on the delay that one additional vehicle on the link imposes on others. Travel time-based congestion pricing set the toll depending on the time it takes to traverse a link. Both schemes help the network get closer to system optimum. These schemes, applied to a future where mode choices between personal vehicles (both conventional and AVs), transit, walking/biking, and SAVs exist, resulted in a 3–4% increase in overall social welfare as opposed to scenarios without pricing. Overall congestion dropped across both the schemes and the revenue earned this way could also be reinvested in the community. Additionally, in countries like the United States, gas tax implemented decades ago is unable to generate enough revenue to keep up with rising infrastructure needs. Eventually, with increase in EV usage, the amount of gas used and, consequently, revenue generated from the gas tax, is bound to diminish. Road pricing can play an important role as an alternate source of revenue.

With all the buzz around DRS, naturally, the next step forward from this study was to compare how a fleet of SAVs with DRS would fare in conjunction with pricing schemes. Gurumurthy et al. (2019) simulated competing modes in a future of SAVs where all travelers were considered potential customers for DRS. DRS, as expected and validated by many studies described earlier, lowered congestion compared to a fleet without DRS thanks to empty seats being put to use. However, when Simoni et al. (2019)'s travel-time-based pricing scheme was applied, more benefits were observed. The fleet of SAVs performed better in terms of AVO (average vehicle occupancy), revenue and overall VMT compared to scenarios without pricing policies. The study did not focus directly into the specifics of the pricing scheme analyzed, but showed the possibility of SAVs operating alongside such pricing policies to improve the system, even when DRS was allowed.

5. Costs of SAV service

Operational viability of a fleet of SAVs or SAEVs forms an important point of discussion in this field of research. However, it is equally important to understand the financial aspect of these services. Ride-hailing services by TNCs these days are not making a profit. A large percentage of the fare revenue goes to the driver. Those that cannot turn a profit will have no market to operate, especially without federal funding like in the case of public transit or Burns et al. (2013) included a cost analysis of the simplistic SAV service that they simulated. Low response times, in the order of seconds, combined with high conventional-vehicle replacement ratios in their study showed that SAVs were feasible at as little as \$0.30–\$0.40 per mile. This is nearly one-tenth the fares that taxis charge (about \$3/mile). Spieser et al. (2014) compared SAVs to personal vehicles (both conventional and autonomous), taking into account the explicit yearly costs (operation, retrofitting, and maintenance included) and value of travel time. SAVs were viable at $0.45 per mile, which was lower than both personal AVs and conventional vehicles. Fagnant and Kockelman (2018) showed that an assumed operating cost of $0.50 per mile would require that the fleet's fare be assessed at about $1.00 per mile for a profitable operation when capital costs and traveler waiting costs were included. Bösch et al. (2018b) developed a detailed cost calculator to piece together the different contributions to the cost of an SAV service. Their study concluded an operational cost range from $0.50 per mile, for SAVs with DRS, to $0.70 per mile for private ride in SAVs, which means that a profitable fare may be close to $1.00 per mile that Fagnant and Kockelman (2018) predicted. Bösch et al. (2018a) further used MATSim to simulate costs assessed in Bösch et al. (2018b) but simultaneously across different modes, such as personal rides, shared rides, and transit. They established the tradeoff between VMT and total delay arising from these services, and suggested that the high costs associated with increased VMT can still be offset by gains from reduced travel times observed with SAV services. This is assuming that AV technology is able to maintain smaller headways resulting in higher effective road capacity.

Similar calculations were carried out for the electric alternative. Many researchers delve into this topic from the angle of marketability as Kang et al. (2016) touched on. Iacobucci et al. (2018) proposed a unique concept that would allow SAEVs to save users money on their electricity bill. The plan revolved around Virtual Power Plants (VPPs), a service popular in Japan that combines many energy sources (with a focus on renewable sources) to supply power to consumers at predetermined levels of demand. This predictable power load reduces stress on the grid and thereby reduces the cost of electrical delivery. The study takes place in Tokyo and generates trips using survey data. It is assumed that enough wind and solar generators can be built to cover all non-EV electrical demand. Diesel generators would be available to keep up with excess electrical demand from the SAEVs. The proposed VPP service would also include bundled SAEV service. The study models scenarios with and without vehicle-to-grid (V2G) connectivity. V2G allows vehicles to discharge power back to the grid to smooth power loads in times of high power demand. They found major cost savings with their VPP, but those were dominated by the savings that come from users not needing to own a car. Their system reduced electricity costs by 32% without V2G and by 75% with V2G. SAEVs significantly increased carbon emissions in the study area. This is partly because Japan's current fleet of mostly hybrids is already relatively efficient, and secondly because SAEVs introduce extra VMT due to empty travel.

Chen et al. (2016) also looked at the prices associated with EVs, vehicle automation, chargers, insurance, maintenance, electricity, and replacement batteries. They found SAEVs would cost about \$0.60–\$0.67 per occupied mile to operate when including 10% profit margins. These vehicles would be used an estimated 131–241 miles per day or 47,000–88,000 miles per year assuming minimal downtime for weekends, maintenance, etc. This is compared to \$0.58 per occupied mile for non-EV SAVs with approximately 94,000 annual miles under the same assumptions. Loeb and Kockelman (2019) followed up Chen et al.'s cost estimates with their more detailed model and a few more cost considerations, such as cleaning, land acquisitions for charging stations and demand-based electricity costs. They estimated a cost of about \$0.59 per occupied SAEV mile compared to \$0.45 per occupied mile for a gasoline SAV fleet. This served to provide a rigorous validation of Chen et al.'s estimates.

Kang et al. (2016) also looked carefully at a many of the same costs considered by Chen et al. (2016) and Loeb and Kockelman (2019), like charger costs, vehicle acquisitions, electricity cost and more. They used these figures to help understand SAVs' level of competition with existing car-sharing service Zipcar. They found a market-based profit-maximizing price of \$2.50 per 10 min driving rate and a membership fee of \$6 per month. Zipcar's prices vary by location, but as of 2019, a typical base membership is \$6–\$ 7 per month and about \$10 per hour (\$1.67 per 10 min), up to 180 miles per day.

6. User perspectives

Research described above has supported the many benefits that SAVs can offer, with recommendations on several different facets of SAV use. However, it is important to realize the public perception of these advanced technologies and policies. This section summaries research conducted on the users' perspective on SAV use.

Bansal and Kockelman's (2018) study conducted in 2016 opened up the discussion on how users perceive future SAV use. Their results show that SAV characteristics persuaded large-family households and disabled users to be inclined toward SAVs even when offered at \$3.00 per mile, comparable to present-day taxis, largely owing to lack of mobility options. However, the average willingness to pay across all groups was low at \$1.00 per mile. The characteristics of those willing to use SAVs showed promise for future market penetration. Haboucha et al. (2017) analyzed a survey that was distributed in Israel and North America on car-ownership and modeled whether people are willing to choose shared vehicles over personal vehicles (both conventional and autonomous). Their results, for the year 2015, observed a well-founded hesitation in switching to AV technology. A majority of users willing to switch to SAVs was found to be younger, and those who tend to spend more time in vehicles. Krueger et al.'s (2016) study focused on the choices between SAVs requested for solo travel and SAVs with DRS. Their study showed that people typically viewed these services as completely different options with completely different values of travel time, as expected and assumed in studies. Their results supported Haboucha et al.'s (2017) finding that younger people are the most likely to adopt SAVs for frequent use.

More recent studies indicate that preferences have changed considerably over time. Quarles and Kockelman (2018) took a closer look at how fares would impact respondents' willingness to use SAVs and DRS. Their results suggested a value of $0.44 per mile maximum willingness to pay (WTP) to frequently use the service, which is much lower than what the service may cost (Bösch et al., 2018b). Gurumurthy and Kockelman (2019) also surveyed people's WTP for SAV and DRS services in 2017. Their models predicted a WTP that was slightly higher on average (at $0.73 per mile), although the share of respondents willing to use the service was low. An elasticity analysis revealed that high usage levels were likely in the future with younger people inclined to use SAVs and opt into DRS. More recently a survey by Stoiber et al. (2019) among Swiss households has shown 61% of respondents prefer SAVs over personal AVs. Perceptions may be continually evolving, and these studies show that there may be a general trend toward SAV usage and DRS. However, more surveys need to be conducted to capture this volatility in preferences.

7. Discussion

This chapter covers the body of literature generated from 2010 to present in the realm of SAVs. SAVs are almost here and researchers around the world have studied several aspects of SAV usage. Table 1 shows a comprehensive list of articles relevant to this review laid out in chronological order. The different aspects of SAVs covered so far in this chapter are listed across the table.

Several frameworks have been developed from scratch to analyze SAV use in different regions. To date, the most widely applied model for SAV

Table 1 Features and contributions of all relevant articles on SAVs.

Relevant articles (chronological)	Region	Dynamic ride-share	Electric vehicles	Large-scale (>1 M trips)	Emissions	Simulation	Optimization	Tolls/ pricing	Cost analysis	User perspective	Parking	First-mile–last-mile
Burns et al. (2013)	3 U.S. cities					✓						
Spieser et al. (2014)	Singapore						✓					
Brownell and Kornhauser (2014)	New Jersey			✓			✓					
Fagnant and Kockelman (2014)	10 mi grid				✓	✓						
Fagnant et al. (2015)	Austin, TX					✓						
Burghout et al. (2015)	Stockholm, Sweden	✓					✓					
Zhang et al. (2015)	10 mi grid										✓	
Bösch et al. (2016)	Zurich, Switzerland			✓		✓						
Bischoff and Maciejewski (2016)	Zurich, Switzerland			✓		✓						
Chen and Kockelman (2016)	100 mi grid		✓			✓			✓			
Haboucha et al. (2017)	Israel and North America									✓		
Krueger et al. (2016)	Australia	✓								✓		

Continued

Table 1 Features and contributions of all relevant articles on SAVs.—cont'd

Relevant articles (chronological)	Region	Dynamic ride-share	Electric vehicles	Large-scale (>1 M trips)	Emissions	Simulation	Optimization	Tolls/ pricing	Cost analysis	User perspective	Parking	First-mile–last-mile
Liang et al. (2016)	Delft, Netherlands											✓
Chen et al. (2016)	100 mi grid		✓			✓			✓			
Kang et al. (2016)	Ann Arbor, MI		✓			✓						
Fagnant and Kockelman (2018) [published online in 2016]	Austin, TX	✓				✓			✓			
Bansal and Kockelman (2018) [published online in 2016]	Texas									✓		
Maciejewski et al. (2017)	—	✓		✓		✓						
Yang et al. (2017)	Shanghai, China		✓			✓						
Hörl (2017)	Sioux Falls, SD	✓		✓		✓						
Heilig et al. (2017)	Stuttgart, Germany	✓		✓		✓						
Zhang and Guhathakurta (2017)	Atlanta, GA			✓		✓					✓	
Martinez and Viegas (2017)	Lisbon, Portugal	✓		✓	✓	✓						

Scheltes and de Almeida Correia (2017)	Delft, Netherlands				✓					✓
Levin et al. (2017)	Austin, TX	✓			✓					
Liu et al. (2017)	Austin, TX			✓	✓					
Sharon et al. (2017)	—				✓		✓			
Gurumurthy and Kockelman (2019) [data from 2017]	U.S.								✓	
Farhan et al. (2018)	Seattle, WA	✓	✓		✓					✓
Hörl et al. (2018)	Zurich, Switzerland	✓		✓	✓	✓				
de Pinto et al. (2018)	Evanston, IL				✓					✓
Loeb et al. (2018)	Austin, TX		✓	✓	✓					
Bösch et al. (2018a)	Zurich, Switzerland							✓		
Quarles and Kockelman (2018)	U.S.								✓	
Hyland and Mahmassani (2018)	Chicago, IL				✓	✓				
Shen et al. (2018)	Singapore	✓			✓					✓
Iacobucci et al. (2018)	Tokyo, Japan		✓			✓				

Continued

Table 1 Features and contributions of all relevant articles on SAVs.—cont'd

Relevant articles (chronological)	Region	Dynamic ride-share	Electric vehicles	Large-scale (>1 M trips)	Emissions	Simulation	Optimization	Tolls/ pricing	Cost analysis	User perspective	Parking	First-mile–last-mile
Farhan and Chen (2018)	Austin, TX	✓	✓			✓	✓					
Bösch et al. (2018b)	Zurich, Switzerland	✓				✓			✓			
Gurumurthy and Kockelman (2018)	Orlando, FL	✓		✓		✓						
Ruch et al. (2018)	San Francisco, CA	✓		✓		✓	✓					
Liu et al. (2018)	Ann Arbor, MI		✓			✓						
Zhao and Kockelman (2018)	Austin, TX			✓				✓	✓			
Simoni et al. (2019)	Austin, TX			✓		✓		✓				
Gurumurthy et al. (2019)	Austin, TX	✓		✓		✓		✓				
Lee and Kockelman (2019)	Austin, TX				✓							
Stoiber et al. (2019)	Switzerland									✓		
Loeb and Kockelman (2019)	Austin, TX	✓	✓	✓		✓			✓			
Millard-Ball (2019)	San Francisco, CA					✓					✓	

simulations (tracking travelers and vehicles) appears to be MATSim. MATSim is open-source and able to run large-scale simulations. Recent code contributions by researchers around the world have enabled simulation of DRS, SAEVs, and advanced pricing policies. Another emerging agent-based modeling tool for SAVs is POLARIS (Auld et al., 2016), as developed by the US Department of Energy's Argonne National Laboratory.

7.1 Future directions

In the near-term, AVs and human-driven vehicles will share the same infrastructure. Some driver apprehension may exist and these interactions need to be studied. Gaps in the rapidly evolving SAV literature also exist for replacing or complementing traditional transit services, including provision of first-mile and last-mile services. Large-vehicle SAVs with DRS is an important area that can be explored further and use of SAVs for commercial applications is largely missing in the literature. Other areas that merit further examination include congestion and parking impacts from SAV services, in combination with strategic SAV-stop placement (for pickups and drop-offs, especially in dense downtowns or other popular destinations), smart road tolling and microtolling (using AVs' smart GPS systems), and vehicle design, to facilitate relatively private travel during DRS services, and route design, to enable deviations for relatively personalized aBus services. The behavioral response to data privacy from connectivity and data generation in AVs may also impact trip outcomes. These are some of the most immediate future research directions.

References

Auld, J., Hope, M., Ley, H., Sokolov, V., Xu, B., Zhang, K., 2016. POLARIS: agent-based modeling framework development and implementation for integrated travel demand and network and operations simulations. Transp. Res. C 64, 101–116. https://doi.org/10.1016/j.trc.2015.07.017.

Bansal, P., Kockelman, K.M., 2018. Are we ready to embrace connected and self-driving vehicles? A case study of Texans. Transportation 45, 641–675. https://doi.org/10.1007/s11116-016-9745-z.

Bischoff, J., Maciejewski, M., 2016. Simulation of city-wide replacement of private cars with autonomous taxis in Berlin. Procedia Comput. Sci. 83, 237–244. https://doi.org/10.1016/j.procs.2016.04.121.

Bösch, P.M., Ciari, F., Axhausen, K.W., 2016. Autonomous vehicle fleet sizes required to serve different levels of demand. Transp. Res. Rec. 2542, 111–119. https://doi.org/10.3141/2542-13.

Bösch, P.M., Ciari, F., Axhausen, K.W., 2018a. Transport policy optimization with autonomous vehicles. Transp. Res. Rec. 2672 0361198118791391. https://doi.org/10.1177/0361198118791391.

Bösch, P.M., Becker, F., Becker, H., Axhausen, K.W., 2018b. Cost-based analysis of autonomous mobility services. Transp. Policy 64, 76–91. https://doi.org/10.1016/j.tranpol.2017.09.005.

Brownell, C., Kornhauser, A., 2014. A driverless alternative: fleet size and cost requirements for a statewide autonomous taxi network in New Jersey. Transp. Res. Rec. 2416, 73–81. https://doi.org/10.3141/2416-09.

Buehler, M., Iagnemma, K., Singh, S. (Eds.), 2009. The DARPA Urban Challenge: Autonomous Vehicles in City Traffic, Springer Tracts in Advanced Robotics. Springer-Verlag, Berlin Heidelberg.

Burghout, W., Rigole, P.-J., Andreasson, I., 2015. Impacts of shared autonomous taxis in a metropolitan area. In: Presented at the 94th Annual Meeting of the Transportation Research Board.

Burns, L.D., Jordan, W.C., Scarborough, B.A., 2013. Transforming Personal Mobility 42. .

Chen, T.D., Kockelman, K.M., 2016. Management of a shared autonomous electric vehicle fleet. Transp. Res. Rec. 2572, 37–46. https://doi.org/10.3141/2572-05.

Chen, T.D., Kockelman, K.M., Hanna, J.P., 2016. Operations of a shared, autonomous, electric vehicle fleet: implications of vehicle & charging infrastructure decisions. Transp. Res. A Policy Pract. 94, 243–254. https://doi.org/10.1016/j.tra.2016.08.020.

Clements, L.M., Kockelman, K.M., 2017. Economic effects of automated vehicles. Transp. Res. Rec. 2606, 106–114. https://doi.org/10.3141/2606-14.

de Pinto, H.K.R.F., Hyland, M.F., Verbas, İ.Ö., Mahmassani, H.S., 2018. Integrated mode choice and dynamic traveler assignment-simulation framework to assess the impact of a suburban first-mile shared autonomous vehicle fleet service on transit demand. In: Presented at the 97th Annual Meeting of the Transportation Research Board. Washington, D.C.

Fagnant, D.J., Kockelman, K.M., 2014. The travel and environmental implications of shared autonomous vehicles, using agent-based model scenarios. Transp. Res. C 40, 1–13. https://doi.org/10.1016/j.trc.2013.12.001.

Fagnant, D.J., Kockelman, K., 2015. Preparing a nation for autonomous vehicles: opportunities, barriers and policy recommendations. Transp. Res. A Policy Pract. 77, 167–181. https://doi.org/10.1016/j.tra.2015.04.003.

Fagnant, D.J., Kockelman, K.M., 2018. Dynamic ride-sharing and fleet sizing for a system of shared autonomous vehicles in Austin, Texas. Transportation 45, 143–158. https://doi.org/10.1007/s11116-016-9729-z.

Fagnant, D.J., Kockelman, K.M., Bansal, P., 2015. Operations of shared autonomous vehicle fleet for Austin, Texas, market. Transp. Res. Rec. 2536, 98–106. https://doi.org/10.3141/2536-12.

Farhan, J., Chen, T.D., 2018. Impact of ridesharing on operational efficiency of shared autonomous electric vehicle fleet. Transp. Res. C 93, 310–321. https://doi.org/10.1016/j.trc.2018.04.022.

Farhan, J., Chen, T.D., Zhang, Z., 2018. Leveraging shared autonomous electric vehicles for first/last mile mobility. In: Presented at the 97th Annual Meeting of the Transportation Research Board. Washington, D.C.

Gurumurthy, K.M., Kockelman, K.M., 2018. Analyzing the dynamic ride-sharing potential for shared autonomous vehicle fleets using cellphone data from Orlando, Florida. Comput. Environ. Urban. Syst. 71, 177–185. https://doi.org/10.1016/j.compenvurbsys.2018.05.008.

Gurumurthy, K.M., Kockelman, K.M., 2019. Modeling Americans' autonomous vehicle preferences: a focus on dynamic ride-sharing, privacy & long-distance mode choices. In: Presented at the 98th Annual Meeting of the Transportation Research Board. Washington, D.C.

Gurumurthy, K.M., Kockelman, K.M., Simoni, M.D., 2019. Benefits and costs of ride-sharing in shared automated vehicles across Austin, Texas: opportunities for congestion pricing. Transp. Res. Rec. 2673, 548–556. https://doi.org/10.1177/0361198119850785.
Haboucha, C.J., Ishaq, R., Shiftan, Y., 2017. User preferences regarding autonomous vehicles. Transp. Res. C 78, 37–49. https://doi.org/10.1016/j.trc.2017.01.010.
Heilig, M., Hilgert, T., Mallig, N., Kagerbauer, M., Vortisch, P., 2017. Potentials of autonomous vehicles in a changing private transportation system—a case study in the Stuttgart region. Transp. Res. Procedia 26, 13–21. https://doi.org/10.1016/j.trpro.2017.07.004.
Hörl, S., 2017. Agent-based simulation of autonomous taxi services with dynamic demand responses. Procedia Comput. Sci. 109, 899–904. https://doi.org/10.1016/j.procs.2017.05.418.
Hörl, S., Ruch, C., Becker, F., Frazzoli, E., Axhausen, K.W., 2018. Fleet control algorithms for automated mobility: a simulation assessment for Zurich. In: Presented at the 97th Annual Meeting of the Transportation Research Board.
Horni, A., Nagel, K., Axhausen, K.W. (Eds.), 2016. The Multi-Agent Transport Simulation MATSim. Ubiquity Presshttps://doi.org/10.5334/baw.
Hyland, M., Mahmassani, H.S., 2018. Dynamic autonomous vehicle fleet operations: optimization-based strategies to assign AVs to immediate traveler demand requests. Transp. Res. C 92, 278–297. https://doi.org/10.1016/j.trc.2018.05.003.
Iacobucci, R., McLellan, B., Tezuka, T., 2018. The synergies of shared autonomous electric vehicles with renewable energy in a virtual power plant and microgrid. Energies 11, 2016. https://doi.org/10.3390/en11082016.
Kang, N., Feinberg, F.M., Papalambros, P.Y., 2016. Autonomous electric vehicle sharing system design. J. Mech. Des. 139, 011402. 011402–10, https://doi.org/10.1115/1.4034471.
Anticipating emissions impacts of smoother driving by connected and autonomous vehicles using MOVES model. Kockelman, K., Boyles, S. (Eds.), 2018. Smart Transport for Cities & Nations: The Rise of Self-Driving & Connected Vehicles. Amazon's Create Space.
Kockelman, K., Boyles, S., Avery, P., Claudel, C., Loftus-Otway, L., Fagnant, D., Bansal, P., Levin, M.W., Zhao, Y., Liu, J., Clements, L., Wagner, W., Stewart, D., Sharon, G., Albert, M., Stone, P., Hanna, J., Patel, R., Fritz, H., Choudhary, T., Li, T., Nichols, A., Sharma, K., Simoni, M., 2016. Bringing Smart Transport to Texans: Ensuring the Benefits of a Connected and Autonomous Transport System in Texas (No. FHWA/TX-16/0-6838-2). TxDOT.
Kockelman, K., Boyles, S., Claudel, C., Stone, P., Loftus-Otway, L., Sturgeon, P., Sharon, G., Gurumurthy, K.M., Huang, Y., Simoni, M., Lei, T., Patel, R., He, D., Mohamed, A., Liu, J., Yarmohammadi, S., Thorn, E., Wagner, W., Stewart, D., Albert, M., Hanna, J., 2018. Phase 2—Bringing Smart Transport to Texans: Ensuring the Benefits of a Connected and Autonomous Transport System in Texas (No. FHWA/TX-18/0–6838-3). TxDOT.
Krueger, R., Rashidi, T.H., Rose, J.M., 2016. Preferences for shared autonomous vehicles. Transp. Res. C 69, 343–355. https://doi.org/10.1016/j.trc.2016.06.015.
Lee, J., Kockelman, K.M., 2019. Energy and emissions implications of self-driving vehicles. In: Presented at the 98th Annual Meeting of the Transportation Research Board. Washington, D.C.
Levin, M.W., Kockelman, K.M., Boyles, S.D., Li, T., 2017. A general framework for modeling shared autonomous vehicles with dynamic network-loading and dynamic ride-sharing application. Comput. Environ. Urban. Syst. 64, 373–383. https://doi.org/10.1016/j.compenvurbsys.2017.04.006.
Liang, X., de Correia, G.H.A., van Arem, B., 2016. Optimizing the service area and trip selection of an electric automated taxi system used for the last mile of train trips. Transport Res E-Log 93, 115–129. https://doi.org/10.1016/j.tre.2016.05.006.

Liu, J., Kockelman, K.M., Bösch, P.M., Ciari, F., 2017. Tracking a system of shared autonomous vehicles across the Austin, Texas network using agent-based simulation. Transportation 44, 1261–1278. https://doi.org/10.1007/s11116-017-9811-1.

Liu, M., Taiebat, M., Xu, M., Hsu, S.-C., 2018. Multiagent spatial simulation of autonomous taxis for urban commute: travel economics and environmental impacts. J. Urban Plann. Dev. 144, 04018033 https://doi.org/10.1061/(ASCE)UP.1943-5444.0000469.

Loeb, B., Kockelman, K.M., 2019. Fleet performance and cost evaluation of a shared autonomous electric vehicle (SAEV) fleet: a case study for Austin, Texas. Transp. Res. A Policy Pract. 121, 374–385. https://doi.org/10.1016/j.tra.2019.01.025.

Loeb, B., Kockelman, K.M., Liu, J., 2018. Shared autonomous electric vehicle (SAEV) operations across the Austin, Texas network with charging infrastructure decisions. Transp. Res. C 89, 222–233. https://doi.org/10.1016/j.trc.2018.01.019.

Maciejewski, M., Bischoff, J., Hörl, S., Nagel, K., 2017. Towards a testbed for dynamic vehicle routing algorithms. In: Bajo, J., Vale, Z., Hallenborg, K., Rocha, A.P., Mathieu, P., Pawlewski, P., … Holmgren, J. (Eds.), Highlights of Practical Applications of Cyber-Physical Multi-Agent Systems, Communications in Computer and Information Science. Springer International Publishing, pp. 69–79.

Martinez, L.M., Viegas, J.M., 2017. Assessing the impacts of deploying a shared self-driving urban mobility system: an agent-based model applied to the city of Lisbon, Portugal. Int. J. Transp. Sci. Technol. 6, 13–27. https://doi.org/10.1016/j.ijtst.2017.05.005.

Millard-Ball, A., 2019. The autonomous vehicle parking problem. Transp. Policy 75, 99–108. https://doi.org/10.1016/j.tranpol.2019.01.003.

Quarles, N.T., Kockelman, K.M., 2018. Americans' Plans for Acquiring and Using Electric, Shared and Self-Driving Vehicles.

Ruch, C., Hörl, S., Frazzoli, E., 2018. AMoDeus, a simulation-based testbed for autonomous mobility-on-demand systems. In: 2018 21st International Conference on Intelligent Transportation Systems (ITSC). Presented at the 2018 21st International Conference on Intelligent Transportation Systems (ITSC). pp. 3639–3644. https://doi.org/10.1109/ITSC.2018.8569961.

Scheltes, A., de Almeida Correia, G.H., 2017. Exploring the use of automated vehicles as last mile connection of train trips through an agent-based simulation model: an application to Delft, Netherlands. Int. J. Transp. Sci. Technol. 6, 28–41. https://doi.org/10.1016/j.ijtst.2017.05.004.

Sharon, G., Levin, M.W., Hanna, J.P., Rambha, T., Boyles, S.D., Stone, P., 2017. Network-wide adaptive tolling for connected and automated vehicles. Transp. Res. C 84, 142–157. https://doi.org/10.1016/j.trc.2017.08.019.

Shen, Y., Zhang, H., Zhao, J., 2018. Integrating shared autonomous vehicle in public transportation system: a supply-side simulation of the first-mile service in Singapore. Transp. Res. A Policy Pract. 113, 125–136. https://doi.org/10.1016/j.tra.2018.04.004.

Simoni, M.D., Kockelman, K.M., Gurumurthy, K.M., Bischoff, J., 2019. Congestion pricing in a world of self-driving vehicles: an analysis of different strategies in alternative future scenarios. Transp. Res. C 98, 167–185. https://doi.org/10.1016/j.trc.2018.11.002.

Spieser, K., Treleaven, K., Zhang, R., Frazzoli, E., Morton, D., Pavone, M., 2014. Toward a systematic approach to the design and evaluation of automated mobility-on-demand systems: a case study in Singapore. In: Meyer, G., Beiker, S. (Eds.), Road Vehicle Automation, Lecture Notes in Mobility. Springer International Publishing, Cham, pp. 229–245. https://doi.org/10.1007/978-3-319-05990-7_20.

Stoiber, T., Schubert, I., Hoerler, R., Burger, P., 2019. Will consumers prefer shared and pooled-use autonomous vehicles? A stated choice experiment with Swiss households.

Transp. Res. Part D: Transp. Environ. 71, 265–282. https://doi.org/10.1016/j.trd.2018.12.019.
Yang, J., Dong, J., Wang, W., 2017. A simulation model for performance analysis of electric autonomous taxi systems. In: Presented at the 96th Annual Meeting of the Transportation Research Board.
Zhang, W., Guhathakurta, S., 2017. Parking spaces in the age of shared autonomous vehicles. Transp. Res. Rec. 2651, 80–91. https://doi.org/10.3141/2651-09.
Zhang, W., Guhathakurta, S., Fang, J., Zhang, G., 2015. Exploring the impact of shared autonomous vehicles on urban parking demand: an agent-based simulation approach. Sustain. Cities Soc. 19, 34–45. https://doi.org/10.1016/j.scs.2015.07.006.
Zhao, Y., Kockelman, K.M., 2018. Anticipating the regional impacts of connected and automated vehicle travel in Austin, Texas. J. Urban Plann. Dev. 144, 04018032. https://doi.org/10.1061/(ASCE)UP.1943-5444.0000463.

CHAPTER FIVE

Carsharing's impact and future

Susan Shaheen*, Adam Cohen, Emily Farrar
McLaughlin Hall, University of California, Berkeley, CA, United States
*Corresponding author: e-mail address: sshaheen@berkeley.edu

Contents

Abstract

Carsharing provides members access to a fleet of autos for short-term use throughout the day, reducing the need for one or more personal vehicles. This chapter reviews key terms and definitions for carsharing, common carsharing business models, and existing impact studies. Next, the chapter discusses the commodification and aggregation of mobility services and the role of Mobility on Demand (MOD) and Mobility as a Service (MaaS) on carsharing. Finally, the chapter concludes with a discussion of how the convergence of electrification and automation is changing carsharing, leading to shared automated and electric vehicle (SAEV) fleets.

Keywords: Carsharing, Shared mobility, Mobility on Demand (MOD), Mobility as a Service (MaaS), Shared automated electric vehicles (SAEVs)

Advances in Transport Policy and Planning, Volume 4
ISSN 2543-0009
https://doi.org/10.1016/bs.atpp.2019.09.002

1. Introduction

Across the globe, innovative and emerging mobility services are offering residents, businesses, travelers, and other users more options for on-demand mobility. In recent years, carsharing has grown rapidly due to changing perspectives toward transportation, car ownership, business and institutional fleet ownership, and urban lifestyles. The principle of carsharing is simple: individuals gain the benefits of private-vehicle use without the costs and responsibilities of ownership. Instead of owning one or more vehicles, a household or business accesses a fleet of shared-use autos on an as-needed basis. Individuals gain access to vehicles by joining an organization that maintains a fleet of cars and light trucks in a network of locations. Generally, participants pay a fee each time they use a vehicle. Carsharing can include three types of service models: (1) roundtrip services (a vehicle is returned to its origin); (2) one-way, station-based services (a vehicle is returned to a different designated station location); and (3) one-way, free-floating services (a vehicle can be returned anywhere within a geographic area).

This chapter is organized into five sections. The first section discusses four different types of carsharing business models. The next section examines the impacts of carsharing. This is followed by a discussion of the commodification and aggregation of transportation services and the relationship between carsharing and Mobility on Demand (MOD) and Mobility as a Service (MaaS). Next, the chapter explores how the convergence of electrification and automation is changing carsharing and might evolve into shared automated and electric vehicle fleets. The chapter concludes with a discussion of these trends and their potential impacts on the carsharing industry.

2. Carsharing business models

Carsharing is enabled through four types of common business models based on the relationship of the service provider and consumer. These business models include: (1) business-to-consumer (B2C); (2) business-to-government (B2G); (3) business-to-business (B2B); and (4) peer-to-peer (P2P).

- *Business-to-Consumer (B2C):* In a B2C model, a carsharing provider offers individual consumers access to a business-owned fleet of vehicles through memberships, subscriptions, user fees, or a combination of pricing models. Examples of B2C carsharing providers include Zipcar and Enterprise CarShare (roundtrip) and SHARE NOW (free-floating one-way).

In October 2016, there were approximately 10.3 million roundtrip and 4.7 million one-way carsharing members worldwide (Shaheen et al., 2018a).

- *Business-to-Government (B2G):* In a B2G model, carsharing providers offer transportation services to a public agency. Pricing may include a fee-for service contract, per-transaction cost, or some other pricing model. Typically, B2G carsharing services are provided by B2C service providers. In the United States (U.S.), the General Services Administration (GSA), an independent agency of the federal government that manages and supports the basic functioning of federal agencies, has authorized the use of carsharing as means to help reduce government expenditures for vehicle fleet ownership and management. At the local level, cities, such as Berkeley and Philadelphia, have become carsharing customers in order to reduce municipal vehicle fleet costs.
- *Business-to-Business (B2B):* In a B2B model, carsharing providers sell business customers access to transportation services either through a fee-for-service or usage fees. The service is typically offered to employees to complete work-related trips. Typically, B2B carsharing services are provided by B2C service providers.
- *Peer-to-Peer (P2P):* In a P2P model (sometimes referred to as personal vehicle sharing), carsharing providers broker transactions among vehicle owners and guests by providing the organizational resources needed to make the exchange possible. Members access vehicles through a direct key transfer from the host (or owner) to the guest (or driver) or through operator-installed, in-vehicle technology that enables unattended access. Pricing and access terms for P2P carsharing services vary, as they are typically determined by vehicle hosts listing their vehicles. The P2P carsharing operator generally takes a portion of the P2P transaction amount in return for facilitating the exchange and providing third-party insurance. Examples of P2P carsharing providers in the U.S. include Turo (formerly RelayRides) and Getaround. For example, Turo takes a 25% commission from the host along with 10% from the guest, and Getaround takes 40% from the host for its services. As of January 2017, 2.9 million members shared 131,336 vehicles as part of a P2P carsharing program in North America (Shaheen et al., 2018b).

An increasing body of anecdotal and empirical evidence indicates that carsharing can provide numerous transportation, land use, environmental, and social benefits. While the impacts of B2C and P2P carsharing models have been more extensively studied, the impacts of B2G and B2B modes have not yet been.

3. Carsharing impacts

Since private vehicles stand idle for an estimated 95% of the time, carsharing can increase the efficiency of automobile use (Fraiberger and Sundararajan, 2015). A number of academic and industry studies have documented the impacts of carsharing, predominantly based on self-reported survey data. However, documenting the comparative impacts of carsharing can be difficult because differences in models, data collection, and study methodologies frequently produce inconsistent results based on limited survey samples and aggregate-level analyses (often attributed to proprietary issues). For these reasons, it can be challenging to provide a comprehensive and unbiased picture. While automated traveler activity data can offer a rich understanding, these data typically do not capture changes in auto ownership, travel behavior across all modes, and respondent perceptions over time. Beyond operator surveys, many large transportation surveys have begun to assess shared mobility, including the American Community Survey and the California Household Travel Survey; nevertheless, these instruments also collect self-reported data. While travel behavior surveys have validity issues, such as respondents exaggerating travel behaviors, underreporting the extent or frequency of travel, inaccurately reporting, and sample bias, they can still offer another source of behavioral understanding (Cohen and Shaheen, 2016). Generally, these academic and industry studies collectively show the following commonly associated outcomes of carsharing:

- Sold vehicles or delayed or foregone vehicle purchases;
- Increased use of some alternative transportation modes (e.g., walking, biking);
- Reduced vehicle miles/kilometers traveled (VMT/VKT);
- Increased access and mobility for formerly carless households;
- Reduced fuel consumption and greenhouse gas (GHG) emissions; and
- Greater environmental awareness.

While the environmental, behavioral, and economic impacts of carsharing services (particularly B2C models) have been well studied, the magnitude of impact varies. Variations in measured impacts can be due to a variety of factors such as: region; density; built environment; public transit accessibility; and carsharing service and business model (e.g., B2C roundtrip, B2C one-way, and P2P). This section reviews and compares existing literature on the impacts of B2C, B2B, and P2P carsharing.

3.1 Impacts of business-to-consumer carsharing

3.1.1 Vehicle ownership

A documented impact of roundtrip carsharing is a reduction in vehicle ownership. Studies and surveys in the U.S. indicate that 11 to 26% of roundtrip carsharing participants sold a personal vehicle and 12 to 68% postponed or entirely avoided a car purchase (Lane, 2005; Martin et al., 2010; Price and Hamilton, 2005). In another study, 30% of City CarShare members in the San Francisco Bay Area shed one or more personal vehicles, and two-thirds chose to postpone the purchase of another vehicle after using the service for two years (Cervero and Tsai, 2004). Several Canadian studies and member surveys suggest that between 15% and 29% of roundtrip carsharing participants sold a vehicle after joining carsharing programs, while 25 to 61% delayed or had forgone a vehicle purchase (Communauto, 2000; Jensen, 2001; Martin et al., 2010). An aggregate-level study of 6281 people in Canada and the U.S. documented 25% of members selling a vehicle due to carsharing and another 25% postponing a vehicle purchase due to roundtrip carsharing (Martin and Shaheen, 2011a). U.S. and Canadian aggregate data also reveal that each roundtrip carsharing vehicle removes between 6 and 23 cars on average from roads (Lane, 2005; Martin et al., 2010; Zipcar, 2005a,b). Martin and Shaheen (2011a) concluded that one carsharing vehicle replaces 9 to 13 vehicles among carsharing members (on average across this aggregate-level study). According to European studies, a carsharing vehicle reduces the need for 4 to 10 privately owned vehicles on average (Rydén and Morin, 2005).

Similar to roundtrip carsharing, studies of one-way carsharing have also documented a reduction in vehicle ownership. A study of free-floating one-way carsharing members across five cities in the U.S. and Canada found that 2 to 5% of participants sold a vehicle after joining carsharing and 8 to 10% on average delayed or had foregone a vehicle purchase (Martin and Shaheen, 2016). This study also found that each free-floating, one-way carsharing vehicle removed 7 to 11 vehicles on average from the road in the cities studied. A study of station-based, one-way carsharing participants in France found a 23% reduction in private-vehicle ownership after joining Autolib' (now defunct) (6t, 2014). The study also found that each Autolib' vehicle removed three private vehicles on average from the road.

Studies of P2P carsharing in North America have also shown reductions in vehicle ownership. Shaheen et al. (2018c) examined three P2P operators and found a 14% reduction in private-vehicle ownership after joining P2P carsharing. P2P services may also suppress vehicle purchases (Shaheen et al., 2018a,c; Dill et al., 2014).

Table 1 provides an examination of the impacts of roundtrip, one-way, and P2P carsharing on vehicle holdings across North America and Europe.

Table 1 Impacts on vehicle holdings.

Operator and location		Source	Number of vehicles removed from the road per carsharing vehicle	Members selling personal vehicle	Members avoiding vehicle purchase
Roundtrip carsharing					
North America					
Arlington carsharing (Flexcar and Zipcar) *Arlington, VA*		Price and Hamilton (2005)		25%	68%
		Price et al. (2006)		29%	71%
Carsharing Portland *Portland, OR*		Katzev (1999)		26%	53%
		Cooper et al. (2000)		23%	25%
City CarShare *San Francisco, CA*	*Year 1*	Cervero (2003)		3%	60%
	Year 2	Cervero and Tsai (2004)	6.8	29%	68%
Modo *Vancouver, Canada*		Namazu and Dowlatabadi (2018)	5	35%	42%[a]/ 62%[b]
PhillyCarshare *Philadelphia, PA*		Lane (2005)	10.8[c]	25%	29%
Short-Term Auto Rental (STAR) *San Francisco, CA*		Walb and Loudon (1986)		15%	43%
Surveyed members of 11 carsharing companies *U.S. and Canada*		Martin and Shaheen (2011b)	9–13	33%	25%
Zipcar *U.S.*		Zipcar (2005a,b)	20	32%	39%

Table 1 Impacts on vehicle holdings.—cont'd

Operator and location	**Source**	**Number of vehicles removed from the road per carsharing vehicle**	**Members selling personal vehicle**	**Members avoiding vehicle purchase**
Europe				
Annual survey of car clubs *London, UK*	Gleave (2017)	11	16%	34%
Flinkster *Berlin and Munich, Germany*	Giesel and Nobis (2016)		15%	
Mobizen *France*	6t (2014)	7	67%	
Moses project *Bremen, Germany and Belgium*	Rydén and Morin (2005)	4–10	21–34%	14–17%
Two providers *Frankfurt am Main, Germany*	Lichtenberg and Hanel (2007)		14%	27%
One-way carsharing				
North America				
car2go *U.S. and Canada*	Martin and Shaheen (2016)	7–11	2–5%	7–10%
car2go *Vancouver, Canada*	Namazu and Dowlatabadi (2018)	6	12%	30%[a]/ 55%[b]
Europe				
Annual survey of car clubs *London, UK*	Gleave (2017)	11	19%	27%
Autolib *France*	6t (2014)	3	23%	
car2go *Ulm, Germany*	Firnkorn and Müller (2011)			14%[d]

Continued

Table 1 Impacts on vehicle holdings.—cont'd

Operator and location	Source	Number of vehicles removed from the road per carsharing vehicle	Members selling personal vehicle	Members avoiding vehicle purchase
DriveNow *Berlin and Munich, Germany*	Giesel and Nobis (2016)		7%	
Free-floating carsharing service *Basel, Switzerland*	Becker et al. (2018)		6%	
Free-floating carsharing service *London, UK*	Le Vine and Polak (2017)		4%	30%
P2P carsharing				
North America				
Getaround, RelayRides (Turo), and eGo carshare *U.S.*	Shaheen et al. (2018c)		14%	19%
Getaround *Portland, OR*	Dill et al. (2014)			44%

[a]Among respondents who did not change vehicle ownership since joining carsharing service.
[b]Among respondents who decreased vehicle ownership since joining carsharing service.
[c]Reflects vehicles removed by members who gave up a car.
[d]Expected impact based on intentions to forgo future purchases.

3.1.2 Modal shift

Roundtrip, one-way, and P2P carsharing also have an impact on modal shift. Tables 2 and 3 provide an overview of North American studies that examine modal shift. The studies vary in the methodology used to probe mode shift. Table 2 contains studies that ask respondents how their travel behavior has changed since joining carsharing, while Table 3 summarizes studies that ask respondents the modes they would use, if carsharing services were not available. Overall, these studies have examined the impact of carsharing on public transit and non-motorized travel. While these studies generally have found a slight overall decline in public transit use, carsharing members exhibited an increase in the use of alternative modes, such as walking. Location-specific

Table 2 Modal shift due to carsharing participation.

Operator and location	Source	Walk		Bike		Use public transit		Take taxis		Drive		Take trips		Carpool/ridesharing		TNCs	
		More often	Less often	More often	Less often	More often	Less often	More often	Less often	More often	Less often	More often	Less often	More often	Less often	More often	Less often
Roundtrip carsharing																	
Arlington Carsharing (Flexcar and Zipcar) *Arlington, VA*	Price and Hamilton (2005)	49%				54%					50%						
	Price et al. (2006)	47%				47%											
Carsharing Portland *Portland, OR*	Cooper et al. (2000)	26%	2%	10%	7%	14%	8%										
North American carsharing *Canada and U.S.*	Martin and Shaheen (2011a)	12%	9%	10%	4%	8% *rail* 12% *bus*	9% *rail* 13% *bus*			4%[a]	15%[a]			5%	2%		
PhillyCarshare *Philadelphia, PA*	Lane (2005)[b]	37%	0%	19%	6%	37%	2%	37%	2%	8%	77%						
	Lane (2005)[c]	6%	2%	3%	6%	4%	12%	2%	27%	48%	14%						

Continued

Table 2 Modal shift due to carsharing participation.—cont'd

Operator and location	Source	Walk		Bike		Use public transit		Take taxis		Drive		Take trips		Carpool/ ridesharing		TNCs	
		More often	Less often	More often	Less often	More often	Less often	More often	Less often	More often	Less often	More often	Less often	More often	Less often	More often	Less often
One-way carsharing																	
car2go *US and Canada*	Martin and Shaheen (2016)	10–34%	9–12%	3–7%	2–8%	3–11% *urban rail* 3–8% *bus* 0–6% *intercity rail*	3–24% *urban rail* 21–48% *bus* 1–5% *intercity rail*	1–3%	42–65%	11–47%	10–27%					6–22%	16–37%
car2go *San Diego, CA*	Shaheen et al. (2018d)	33%	9%			12%	24%	2%	59%	11%	26%					22%	17%
P2P carsharing																	
Getaround, RelayRides (Turo), and eGo Carshare *U.S.*	Shaheen et al. (2018c)	15%	2%	10% *personal bike* 3% *public bikesharing*	3% *personal bike* 3% *public bikesharing*	7% *urban rail* 9% *bus*	8% *urban rail* 10% *bus*	4%	15%			37%	8%	11%	5%	9%	9%

[a]Change in mode use for commuting.
[b]Members who reduced their car ownership.
[c]Members who gained access to a car.

Table 3 If carsharing was discontinued, what modes would household use in its place?

Operator and location	Source	Walk	Bike	Use public transit	Take taxis	Drive personal vehicle	Take trips	Carpool	Other carsharing service	Rental car	Borrow a car from a family member
Roundtrip carsharing											
Modo *Vancouver*	Namazu and Dowlatabadi (2018)	15%	13%	41%	32%	24%	27% would have taken fewer trips	16%			
TCRP Report—surveyed members of more than nine carsharing companies *North America*	Millard-Ball et al. (2005)	15%		39%	34%			36%			
One-way carsharing											
car2go *Vancouver*	Namazu and Dowlatabadi (2018)	25%		57%	44%	46%	15% would have taken fewer trips				
P2P carsharing											
Getaround *Portland, OR*	Dill et al. (2014)	0%[a]	2%[a]	20%[a]		3%[a]	33% would not have made the trip*	8%[a]	12%[a]	7%[a]	14%[a]

[a]Without Getaround, how would you have made this trip previously?

variations—including urban density, public transit service and availability, socio-demographics, and cultural norms—contribute to these modal shifts, and they are likely to result in varying impacts depending on the specific context carsharing is deployed.

In France, the French national survey comparing roundtrip and station-based, one-way carsharing showed differing impacts on modal shift (6t, 2014). The study found that both forms of carsharing reduced private-vehicle use, with roundtrip carsharing having a greater reduction impact. The study also found that roundtrip carsharing increased public transit use slightly, whereas station-based, one-way carsharing reduced it. While the study found that both forms of carsharing reduced private bicycle use, roundtrip carsharing increased bikesharing ridership.

3.1.3 Vehicle miles/kilometers traveled

A reduction in vehicle ownership may result in lowered VMT/VKT, reduced parking demand, and increased use of other transport modes (such as cycling and walking) in lieu of vehicle travel. Carsharing is thought to lead to lower VMT/VKT by emphasizing variable driving costs, such as per hour and/or mileage charges (Shaheen et al., 2006). Reductions range from as little as 3% to as much as 80% of a member's total VMT/VKT on average in Canada and the U.S. for roundtrip carsharing; estimates differ notably between members who gave up vehicles after joining carsharing programs and those that gained vehicle access through carsharing (Cervero, 2003; Cooper et al., 2000; Lane, 2005; Zipcar, 2005a,b). European studies of roundtrip carsharing also indicate a large reduction in VKT ranging from 28 to 45% on average (Shaheen and Cohen, 2007). Martin et al. (2010) also documented roundtrip carsharing reductions in VMT/VKT from 27 to 43% in the U.S. and Canada. One-way studies have also documented reductions in VMT/VKT. The study of one-way, station-based carsharing in France documented an 11% reduction in VKT (6t, 2014). A study of free-floating, one-way carsharing in the U.S. and Canada found VMT/VKT reductions ranging from 6% (in Calgary, Alberta) to 16% (in Vancouver, British Columbia, and Washington, DC) (Martin and Shaheen, 2016). This percentage reduction considers an estimate of the total driving by households on average, as derived from annual VMT/VKT responses and broader reductions in driving computed for the population. Table 4 provides a summary of studies that examine changes in VMT/VKT.

Reduced vehicle ownership rates and VMT/VKT can also lead to lower GHG emission levels, as trips are shifted to other modes. In Europe,

Table 4 Impacts on VMT/VKT.

Operator and location		Authors, year	Percent VMT/VKT change per member
Roundtrip carsharing			
Arlington carsharing (Flexcar and Zipcar) *Arlington, VA*		Price and Hamilton (2005)	−40
		Price et al. (2006)	−43
Carsharing Portland *Portland, OR*		Cooper et al. (2000)	−7.6
City CarShare *San Francisco, CA*	*Year 1*	Cervero (2003)	−3 for members −58 for non-members
	Year 2	Cervero and Tsai (2004)	−47 for members +73 for non-members
	Year 4	Cervero et al. (2007)	−67 for members +24 for non-members
Moses project *Europe*		Rydén and Morin (2005)	−28 to −45
PhillyCarshare *Philadelphia, PA*		Lane (2005)	−42
TCRP report—surveyed members of more than nine carsharing companies *North America*		Millard-Ball et al. (2005)	−63
Surveyed members of 11 carsharing companies *U.S. and Canada*		Martin et al. (2010)	−27
Zipcar *U.S.*		Zipcar (2005a,b)	−80
One-way carsharing			
car2go *U.S. and Canada*		Martin and Shaheen (2016)	−6 to −16

carsharing is estimated to reduce the average user's carbon dioxide (CO_2) emissions by 40 to 50% (Stockholm, 2005). The estimated change in emissions was calculated for Bremen, Germany and Belgium based on change in car mileage, vehicles used, and public transport usage; the results are available in Table 5. In an aggregate study across North American cities, Martin and

Table 5 Reductions in CO_2 emissions.
The estimated total change in emissions of CO_2

	Belgium	Bremen
Change in car mileage	−28%	−45%
Change in vehicles used	−17%	−17%
Change in public transport usage	+2%	+2%
Total	−39%	−54%

Adapted from Rydén, C. Morin, E., 2005. Mobility services for urban sustainability. Environmental Assessment. Report WP 6. Trivector Traffic AB, Stockhom, Sweden. 213.170.188.3/moses/Downloads/reports/del_6.pdf.

Shaheen (2011b) estimated an average GHG emission reduction of 34 to 41% per household or an average reduction of 0.58 to 0.84 metric tons per household for roundtrip carsharing. Studies of free-floating, one-way carsharing estimate that each car2go vehicle reduced GHG emissions by 4% (Calgary) to 18% (Washington, DC) on average (Martin and Shaheen, 2016). In addition, many carsharing organizations include low-emission vehicles—such as electric, plug-in hybrid, and gasoline-electric hybrid cars—in their fleets; use of these vehicle types can result in additional GHG emission decreases. Carsharing members also report a higher degree of environmental awareness after joining a carsharing program (Lane, 2005).

3.1.4 Social impacts

Finally, empirical evidence demonstrates that carsharing has a range of beneficial social impacts. Households can gain or maintain access to vehicles without bearing the full costs of car ownership. Depending on the location and the organization operating the carsharing program, the maximum user mileage where carsharing is more cost effective (in comparison to owning or leasing a personal vehicle) is between 6200 and 10,000 miles (Shaheen et al., 2006). In comparison, the average U.S. household drives approximately 13,500 miles annually (Office of Highway Policy Information, 2018). Low-income households and college students can also benefit from participation in carsharing programs (Stocker et al., 2016). Numerous studies of roundtrip carsharing in North America have found that carsharing households saved an average of US$154 to $435 per month compared to private-vehicle use (Shaheen et al., 2012).

3.2 Impacts of business-to-business carsharing

Businesses can also enroll in carsharing and provide mobility options for their employees. Studies of the impacts of B2B carsharing are limited. Shaheen and Stocker (2015) conducted a survey of 23,774 active North American Zipcar members, 523 of which were identified as corporate members. At the time of the study in 2014, business members comprised approximately one quarter of the North American Zipcar membership. The study found that business carsharing can be a gateway to personal carsharing use. The study found that one-fifth of corporate users surveyed claimed to have sold a vehicle and another fifth claimed to have postponed purchasing a vehicle due to joining carsharing through their employers. After joining carsharing, corporate members overall reported biking and taking public transit slightly less often and walking slightly more often. However, among the subset of corporate members who sold or postponed a vehicle purchase due to carsharing, respondents reported taking public transit and walking more often. See Fig. 1.

Fig. 2 displays mode replacement for corporate Zipcar members. If carsharing were not available, many of the corporate member respondents claimed they would have used a car rental company or driven a personal or borrowed vehicle. There is a 13% induced demand effect (trips taken that would not have occurred, if carsharing was not present), as 11% of respondents claim they would not have made the trip at all, and 2% claim they would have accomplished the task online (e.g., online shopping).

The study found that business carsharing can change a member's likelihood to buy/lease a personal car within the next few years. Forty-nine percent of respondents claimed they are less likely to buy a car in the near future since joining carsharing, and 41% reported their likelihood had not changed (Shaheen and Stocker, 2015).

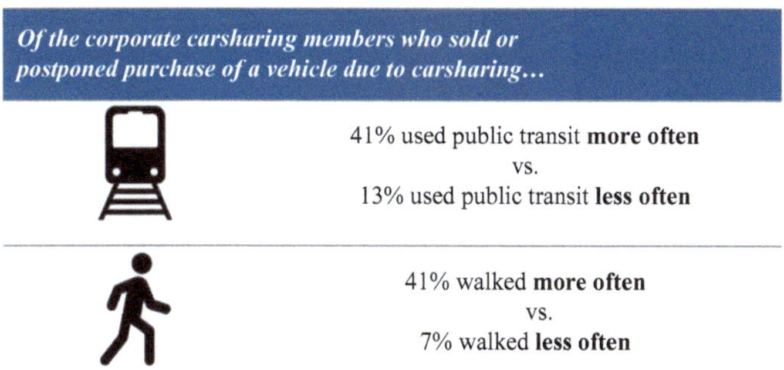

Fig. 1 Travel behavior impacts for B2B members who sold or postponed purchasing a vehicle.

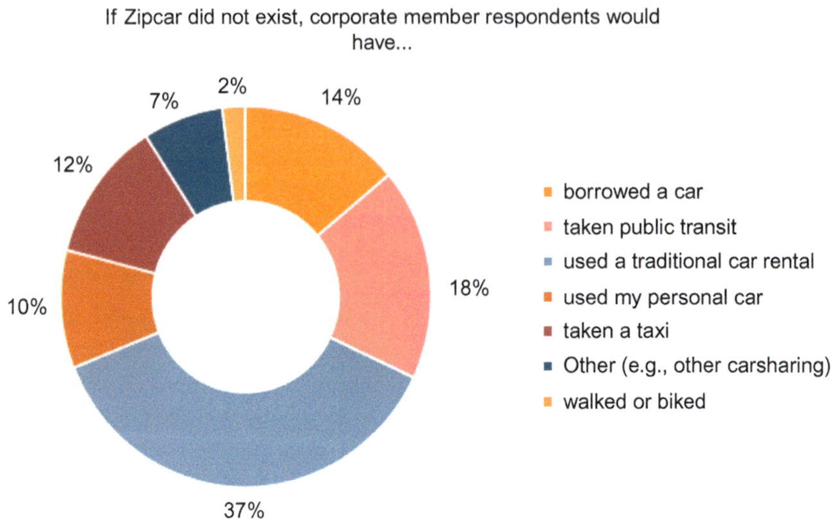

Fig. 2 B2B carsharing mode replacement.

3.3 Impacts of peer-to-peer carsharing

A few studies have examined the impacts of P2P carsharing. Shaheen et al. (2018c) found that P2P carsharing encourages some households to reduce, delay, or even avoid a vehicle purchase. Additionally, the services offer individuals the opportunity to drive a variety of vehicle types. P2P carsharing also enables hosts to reduce their ownership costs, monetize otherwise idle assets, or both. Shaheen et al. (2018c) surveyed 1151 guests and hosts from three U.S. P2P carsharing programs and documented four key findings:

- *Vehicle Ownership*: Most P2P carsharing members (46%) were from carless households that joined P2P carsharing to gain additional mobility. Another 20% enrolled to earn money sharing their vehicle, while 14% of respondents indicated that they held off on a vehicle purchase due to their carsharing membership. A small percentage (3%) noted that they had sold a vehicle because of their membership.
- *Ease of Use*: Forty-eight percent of respondents felt that P2P carsharing was easier than expected to use compared to 15% who said that vehicle sharing was more challenging to use than anticipated. These findings may suggest that more education and outreach could help to expand the use of P2P carsharing to new users.

- *Changes to Travel Modes*: Most respondents reported no major change in their public transit use as a result of P2P carsharing, with 9% increasing bus ridership and 10% decreasing it. Similarly, 7% of respondents reported increasing rail use, while 8% reported a decrease. Taxi use showed a net decline among all respondents. Survey respondents that use transportation network companies (TNCs, also known as ridesourcing and ridehailing), such as Lyft and Uber, were split—as 9% reported an increase and another 9% noted a decrease. In contrast, carpooling showed a net increase (6%) among the sample, suggesting that P2P carsharing users were likely traveling with multiple occupants.
- *Super Sharers:* In addition, P2P carsharing was used in conjunction with other shared-mobility services. Respondents reported that 14% were members of at least one other P2P carsharing service, 43% were members of at least one other carsharing organization, and 78% had used at least one other shared service. Many P2P carsharing members were also frequent Lyft and Uber users, broadly suggesting that they used a portfolio of shared modes to meet their transportation needs.

Additionally, the study also unveiled motivations and barriers for using P2P carsharing. For vehicle owners, key opportunities and motivations included: (1) earning revenue on existing, often underused vehicles and (2) contributing to the "sharing economy" by providing mobility access to others. Common barriers for vehicle owners included: (1) concerns about their inability to use their personal vehicle when it is accessed by a guest, (2) potential vehicle damage, and (3) complex insurance requirements that vary by jurisdiction.

For vehicle guests, key opportunities and motivations to participate in P2P carsharing include: (1) accessing a wide array of vehicles, including luxury and zero-emission models and (2) avoiding the costs and hassles associated with private-vehicle ownership such as: parking, maintenance, and insurance. Common barriers for vehicle owners include: (1) first/last-mile connections to access P2P carsharing vehicles, (2) key pick-up and drop-off, and (3) lack of reliable response from a car host following a sharing request. Access to/from vehicles and other challenges suggest expanding P2P carsharing outside of urban areas could be more challenging.

Other studies have focused on the impacts of P2P carsharing on low-income household vehicle access. A study of P2P carsharing use in Portland, Oregon found that 37% of families in poverty live in a census block group that contains at least one P2P vehicle, but only 13% live in a census block that has a roundtrip carsharing vehicle. In parts of East Portland, which is a lower-income area of Portland, P2P vehicles are the only type of carsharing vehicles available (Dill et al., 2014). Further, Fraiberger and Sundararajan (2015) project that P2P carsharing will have more pronounced impacts on below-median income consumers than above-median income users. Fraiberger and Sundararajan (2015) found that below-median income households are almost twice as likely to give up private-vehicle ownership attributable to their greater propensity to avoid the fixed costs of private-vehicle ownership when a peer-to-peer carsharing alternative exists.

4. Carsharing and the commodification and aggregation of mobility services

Mobility needs, consumption, and travel behavior are changing (Galinsky, 2016; Koettl, 2016; Kolko, 2017; Reagan and Picker, 2017; Shaheen and Cohen, 2018b). Increasingly, consumers are assigning economic values to modes and engaging in multimodal decisionmaking based on a variety of factors including: cost, travel time, wait time, number of connections, convenience, and other attributes. Rather than making decisions between modes, mobility consumers can make decisions among modes, in essence "modal chaining" to optimize route, travel time, and cost. These changes are contributing to the growth of commodified and aggregated mobility services, as well as multimodal carsharing (e.g., one-way carsharing as a link to public transit). While carsharing can be employed independently of other services, enabling technologies, like smartphone apps, and the presence of other shared modes (e.g., bikesharing, scooter sharing, etc.) can increase the effectiveness and potential benefits of carsharing by creating a "network effect," where mobility options in close proximity to one another can add collective value.

4.1 Mobility on Demand (MOD) in the U.S.

In the U.S., consumers are assessing transportation services by considering their economic and hedonic values in making mobility decisions (including the decision not to travel and instead having a good or service delivered) based on cost, travel and wait time, number of connections, convenience, and other attributes. This concept is also known as Mobility on Demand (MOD) and Mobility as a Service (MaaS). The U.S. Department of Transportation and Federal Transit Administration are funding pilots and research as part of their MOD Sandbox program to explore partnerships; developing new business models; integrating public transit and MOD strategies; and investigating emerging technical capabilities such as: integrated payment systems, decision support, incentives for traveler choices, and supply and demand management of the transportation network. For example, the Tri-County Metropolitan Transportation District of Oregon (TriMet) is developing a multimodal trip planner that incorporates carsharing, bikesharing, TNCs, and other mobility services as a grantee of the MOD Sandbox program. With MOD, there is also recognition that digital and goods delivery services can substitute for trips, while simultaneously creating demand for new and different trip types.

4.2 Mobility as a Service (MaaS) in Europe

In Europe, services that allow travelers to sign up for mobility services in one package are gaining popularity. The concept of MaaS evolved approximately a decade ago with an initial pilot in Gothenburg, Sweden known as UbiGo. UbiGo operated as a pilot between November 2013 and April 2014. UbiGo repackaged existing transportation services (e.g., public transit, taxi, bikesharing, and carsharing) into a one-stop, monthly, paid subscription service for the entire household (including children) ranging from US$185 to $280 per month for many households (Sochor et al., 2016). This pilot included 195 people (173 adult participants and 22 children under the age of 18 years old). The pilot program contributed to a reduction in household-vehicle ownership and increased use of bikesharing, carsharing, public transportation, and taxis. Based on a self-reported survey of other available modes, 50% of participants walked, 16% used a private bicycle, and 9% used a private vehicle at least three to five times per week (Sochor et al., 2016). More recently, UbiGo relaunched with another pilot in Stockholm in March 2018; the findings of this pilot have not yet been released.

MaaS redistributes the mobility chain by integrating the products and services of mobility providers and supplying them to users as a single service. Typically, a digital platform creates and manages trips that users pay for via a single account. Key features of MaaS include bundled pricing and monthly subscription plans that best fit a user's or household's needs. These bundles and subscriptions can include a certain amount of each transportation service (e.g., carsharing, shared micromobility [bikesharing and scooter sharing], taxis, public transportation, etc.) and are similar to other service bundles, such as mobile-phone plans, where the user pays one price for a combination of multiple service elements (e.g., talk, text, data, roaming, long distance, etc.).

MaaS services often broker travel with suppliers, repackage, and resell it as a bundled package. Generally, there is an emerging consensus that both MOD and MaaS are about integrating multiple transportation modes into a seamless user experience, often necessitating open data and cooperation by public and private transportation stakeholders. With MaaS, there is a strong emphasis on information and fare-payment integration through a single digital platform. Digital information and fare-payment integration, enabled through smartphone apps that are coupled with commodified mobility services, are making traveler options more convenient and seamless. In the future, the convergence of carsharing, electrification, and automation could have transformative effects on mobility, including carsharing.

4.3 The role of vertical and horizontal integration in mobility aggregation

Increasingly, the public and private sectors are employing a variety of horizontal and vertical integration strategies. With vertical integration, a private company provides an app and access to multiple mobility services owned and operated by that company on a single platform (e.g., Uber, UberPOOL, UberEats, Uber Copter, etc.). With horizontal integration, a service provider (either public or private) offers multiple modes and service providers on the same app platform (e.g., Transit App). Some platforms are blending vertical and horizontal integration approaches together, such as Free2Move, which offers its own carsharing service and mobility aggregator with other service providers. Fig. 3 provides an example of

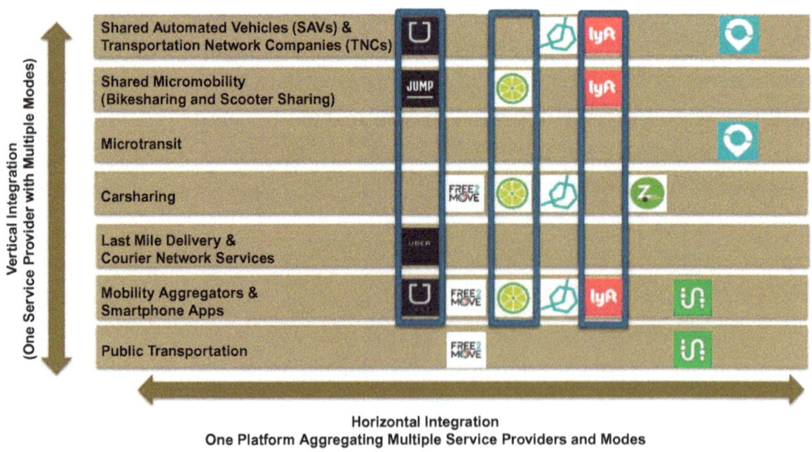

Fig. 3 Examples of vertical and horizontal integration among mobility providers.

these horizontal and vertical integration processes across eight service providers in the shared-mobility sector.

On both sides of the Atlantic, two complementary approaches—MOD and MaaS—have emerged in parallel, each concentrating on providing multimodal access to public and private transportation services. While definitions and understanding of MOD and MaaS are still evolving, MOD focuses on the commodification of passenger mobility and goods delivery and transportation systems management, whereas MaaS focuses primarily on passenger mobility aggregation, integrated fare payment, and subscription services.

5. Carsharing and the future of mobility: Electrification and automation

The convergence of electrification and automation with carsharing is predicted to have a transformative effect on the industry. Vehicle electrification and automation have the potential to reduce GHG emissions and reduce private-vehicle ownership in favor of shared automated vehicles (SAVs).

5.1 Vehicle electrification

Carsharing vehicles that use electricity as their sole source of propulsion powered by clean energy can further reduce air pollutants and GHG emissions, mitigating many of the transportation-related impacts associated with vehicle travel. Lower pollution and maintenance requirements are contributing to increased investment, improved range, and the growing popularity of electric vehicles (EVs).

Estimates indicate that shared and non-shared commercial fleets account for approximately 30% of the market for new EVs as of 2016 (Biondi et al., 2016). In 2017, the global EV market reached 1.2 million vehicles sold, with more than 165 models available for purchase. Based on manufacturer commitments, 25 million EV units are expected to be sold by 2025 (Frost and Sullivan, 2018). Global EV sales were around 1.3% in 2017, up from 0.8% in 2016 (Hertzke et al., 2018). Currently, battery electric vehicles (BEVs) make up 66% of the global EV market, and BEV sales are expected to grow more rapidly than plug-in hybrid electric vehicle (PHEV) sales (Hertzke et al., 2018). China has the largest EV market (larger than the U.S. and Europe combined); however, only Norway has reached a critical mass for EV adoption. In Norway, BEVs accounted for 58% of all car sales in

March 2019 (Norwegian Electric Vehicle Association). While the market for EVs is growing rapidly, market growth is constrained by the availability of charging infrastructure. Charging infrastructure tends to have greater availability in denser regions where EV sales are the highest (Frost and Sullivan, 2018). In recent years, a growing number of ultrafast-charging networks (i.e., stations that charge vehicles in under 10 minutes) have been installed worldwide, particularly in China, Europe, and North America (Eckhouse et al., 2019; Holder, 2019; Kane, 2018; Kummer, 2019; McPhee, 2019; Nicholas and Hall, 2018; Plungis, 2019).

While data on EV penetration in carsharing fleets is limited, anecdotal evidence suggests that EV carsharing fleets are growing. A few popular EV carsharing services include:

- Zipcar Flex—a free-floating carsharing service comprised of approximately 300 EVs in London, UK.
- Car2go, DriveNow, and ReachNow recently joined forces to become SHARE NOW (announced in February 2019)—a joint venture between Daimler AG and BMW Group that consists of a connected ecosystem of five mobility strategies: (1) one-way carsharing, (2) TNCs, (3) multimodal trip planning, (4) parking, and (5) charging. The service includes more than 20,000 carsharing vehicles worldwide (including 3200 EVs) in 30 cities and 13 countries. Ten percent of ReachNow's fleet is electric with 720,000 EV miles driven in less than two years. The company reports that 25% of members have driven EVs, which have saved more than 200 tons of CO_2. Car2go previously operated an all-electric carsharing program in San Diego, California between 2014 and 2016. The program closed due to a number of EV logistical challenges, including insufficient public charging infrastructure and difficulties managing a centralized charging depot that required staff intensive shuttling and rebalancing of the carsharing fleet (Shaheen et al., 2018d).

EV carsharing has the potential to reduce vehicle and GHG emissions, particularly if charged by a clean-power grid. However, operating an EV carsharing program can present a number of unique challenges that may make it more difficult to manage than a carsharing fleet comprised of conventional vehicles. Common logistical challenges can include: reduced driving ranges, increased vehicle downtime (due to charge times), and limited charging infrastructure. For these reasons, while EV carsharing tends to be more sustainable, it also can present notable operational challenges. Carsharing also offers users an opportunity to experience an EV without making a personal investment. EVs can be attractive for many forms of shared modes due to shorter trips, given the limited range of EVs, which can often be parked at charging stations while waiting for the next user. The use of EVs in carsharing fleets faces many challenges both operational (e.g., the cost and logistics of operating an electric fleet, maintaining charging infrastructure, ensuring vehicles remain profitable as charging time typically results in a vehicle being in non-revenue status, etc.) and behavioral (e.g., lack of exposure, range anxiety, and lack of incentives).

Operational challenges associated with carsharing fleets include:

(1) Ensuring sufficient vehicle charge for trip completion,

(2) Maintaining a well-distributed fleet over the service area, and

(3) Balancing fleet and relocation staff size.

To ensure users encounter vehicles with sufficient battery charge to complete their trip, operators must consider the trade-off between the cost of long-term infrastructure (such as charging stations) and the cost of day-to-day operations (Zhao et al. 2018). For example, it may be more cost effective to install additional charging stations, if it means reducing the need for vehicle relocation. Carsharing operators should also consider charging infrastructure location design, such as placing more charging spaces at locations with high vehicle turnover or using a mix of slow- and fast-charging stations.

Maintaining a well-distributed fleet is crucial to operations; if a customer has difficulty finding a vehicle or must walk away due to insufficient charging levels, the experience could have a long-term effect on their perception of the service and willingness to use it in the future. There are several strategies to maintain a well-distributed fleet:

- Vehicle rebalancing,
- Imposing parking reservation policies, and
- Balancing station capacities (Nourinejad et al., 2015).

EV fleets make vehicle rebalancing more difficult and costly due to limited infrastructure and long charging times (Chow, 2018). Carsharing operators should ensure that users find vehicles nearby and have a sufficient charge for tripmaking. Vehicle rebalancing involves logistical challenges, such as the trade-off between designing fleet size and staff size for relocations. A larger fleet means fewer relocations and thus fewer staff are needed, while a smaller fleet involves more intensive vehicle relocation operations (Nourinejad et al., 2015). Naturally, EV fleets necessitate familiarity with electric drive maintenance and operations among staff, perhaps requiring staff retraining.

Car2go in San Diego highlights a few of these EV logistical challenges. In San Diego, car2go began operating a centralized charging depot to charge their vehicles in their second year of operation due to insufficient public charging infrastructure. At the time, this system was the only EV, one-way carsharing system with instant access (i.e., accessible without reservation) operating in the U.S. When a vehicle became depleted, car2go staff would regularly shuttle vehicles from their location back to the charging depot for recharging and then back to the service region. Recognizing these challenges, car2go sought to test different pricing and user incentives to reduce the fleet rebalancing and charging required by program staff (Shaheen et al., 2018d).

Car2go tested two different pricing/incentive structures for their members to improve system operational efficiency (vehicle redistribution, state-of-charge management, use of vehicles placed at public transit stations) and encourage use. The study tested two incentives, each aimed at achieving separate goals:

(1) *Charging:* Reducing the need for staff to retrieve and redistribute vehicles between the central charging station and the service area; and.

(2) *Rebalancing:* Managing supply and demand (e.g., preventing an over-supply of vehicles in low-demand areas).

The first incentive was designed to encourage existing customers to deviate slightly from their intended destination to position the vehicles in a more convenient location for recharging by offering 10 minutes of driving credit to park within a nine-square block zone (Shaheen et al., 2018d).

The rebalancing incentive provided users with a 10-minute driving credit, if they drove a vehicle starting within two predefined regions for at least 10 minutes and parked outside the zone. This incentive was designed to defray user costs as opposed to allowing the member to earn (or accumulate) credits. A member could only receive a credit for an amount of driving that was equivalent to or less than what they had done in an attempt to influence where the vehicles were parked (Shaheen et al., 2018d).

The charging incentive was available to any vehicle in the system whereas the second incentive only applied to vehicles starting in low travel-demand zones. Researchers conducted a total of three surveys to evaluate how car2go members responded to the incentives. The first survey was administered before the start of the incentives, the second following the conclusion of the first incentive, and the final survey was conducted at the conclusion of the study (following the second incentive) (Shaheen et al., 2018d).

The study found that 72% of the sample was aware of the charging incentive prior to taking the survey. Of those, 22% (~16% of the total sample) received the driving credit. Respondents who had not taken advantage of the incentive, but had known about it, were asked why they had not used it. Forty-three percent said that their final destination was rarely within this zone. Among the respondents that received the charging incentive, over 85%, were satisfied with it. Thirty percent of all respondents also reported that they noticed the vehicles had more charge than average after the incentive took effect (Shaheen et al., 2018d). With respect to the rebalancing incentive, only 7% of respondents indicated that they definitely would position a vehicle outside the zone for a 10-minute driving credit. With a credit of 30 minutes, 65% stated that they would reposition the vehicles (Shaheen et al., 2018d).

Overall, respondents generally preferred user credits (e.g., driving minutes) instead of a cash incentive. Eighty-two percent reported that they definitely or probably would have driven a vehicle to the charging zone in downtown San Diego in exchange for a 30-minute driving credit compared to 67% for an equivalent US$12 cash incentive (Shaheen et al., 2018d). Respondents indicated that increasing the incentive amount and extending the date when driving credits expired would induce additional users to take advantage of the incentive program (Shaheen et al., 2018d).

While the incentives changed behavior for some respondents, the incentive amount may not have been large enough to cause considerable behavioral changes to significantly impact operations. However, given the right value, members would change their travel behavior to meet the objectives of the incentive policy (in this case an incentive to offset staff time associated with fleet rebalancing and charging). The study results indicate that transportation incentives can be an effective model for encouraging certain behaviors, such as increasing EV charging and encouraging user rebalancing. Additional experimentation and study may lead to greater operational improvements and understanding for leveraging incentive programs in shared-mobility services (Shaheen et al., 2018d).

5.2 Vehicle automation

In addition to electrification, vehicle automation has the potential to reshape the business of carsharing. SAE International, a global mobility standards organization, has established five levels of vehicle automation:

- Level 1 describes vehicles that automate only one primary control function (e.g., self-parking or adaptive cruise control).
- Level 2 describes a vehicle with automated systems that provides full control of specific functions such as: accelerating, braking, and steering.

With Level 2, the driver must still monitor driving and be prepared to immediately resume control at any time.
- Level 3 includes vehicles that handle situations requiring an immediate response; however, the driver must still be prepared to intervene within a limited amount of time when prompted.
- Level 4 automation has a human operator that does not need to control the vehicle as long as it is operating under the specific conditions the vehicle was intended to function.
- Level 5 describes vehicles capable of driving in all environments without human control.

As Level 4 and 5 automated vehicles (AVs) become more mainstream, it is possible that the B2C and P2P carsharing business models may converge with for-hire services (e.g., taxis and TNCs) to create a new model comprised of shared automated electric vehicles (SAEVs). In 2016, GM invested in both Lyft and Uber, enabling drivers from both to rent for-hire vehicles through its Maven carsharing platform (Swigonski, 2017). Because an SAEV network at scale will be driverless, there will no longer be a need to distinguish between "for-hire" and other vehicle services, such as carsharing and car rental. In the future, the most important distinguishing factor may entail who owns the AV and owns/operates the network or platform where the vehicles are shared (e.g., AVs shared as part of a B2C company vs a privately owned P2P fleet).

A number of studies have attempted to model the potential impacts of SAEVs; however, these studies do not always account for nuances in business models, vehicle ownership, the built environment, public transit accessibility, urban density, and other factors. Thus, predicting generalizable potential impacts of SAEVs is challenging. Table 6 provides a summary of the current modeling literature on the expected environmental impacts of large-scale SAEV deployments. In general, these studies have found that SAEV fleets could: (1) reduce vehicle emissions compared to gasoline-powered fleets, (2) replace privately owned vehicles, and (3) require less charging infrastructure than previously anticipated particularly when EVs are shared.

While the impacts of vehicle automation are uncertain, driverless vehicles will likely result in fundamental changes to public transportation by altering the built environment, costs, commute patterns, and modal choice. Reduced vehicle ownership due to SAVs could result in changes in parking needs and create new opportunities for infill development and increased densities. While SAVs may compete with public transit ridership, infill

Table 6 Impacts of shared automated and electric vehicles (SAEVs).

Publication	Methods	Expected impacts
Greenblatt and Saxena (2015)	Estimated per-mile GHG emissions of a fleet of SAEVs	• SAEV fleet emissions expected to be 87–94% lower than a fleet of 2014 conventional gasoline vehicles • SAEV fleet emissions expected to be 63–82% lower than a fleet of projected 2030 HEVs
Chen et al. (2016)	Modeled management of a fleet of SAEVs under various charging infrastructure and vehicle range scenarios	• Fleet size is dependent upon battery recharging time and vehicle range • An 80-mile range SAEV could replace 3.7 privately owned vehicles • A 200-mile range SAEV could replace 5.5 privately owned vehicles • Faster charging equipment could increase vehicle shedding
Biondi et al. (2016)	Optimized parking location and capacity for a carsharing service with an EV fleet	• Most charging stations would require less than four spots • Only a few large charging stations (up to 15 spots) are needed to be placed in areas of high turnover • Possible impact on peak electricity demand can be mitigated by using fast-charging technologies
Fagnant and Kockelman (2018)	Simulate dynamic ridesharing (DRS) in a SAV fleet for early adopters. Estimates average service times, travel costs, VMT change, and fleet operator earnings[a]	• Without any ridesharing, a SAV fleet could increase VMT by over 8% for its users • With DRS, a fleet of SAVs could increase VMT by 4.5% • Overall VMT may be reduced as SAV membership rises and/or DRS users become more flexible in their trip timing and routing
Gurumurthy et al. (2019)	Simulated travel patterns in Austin, TX in the presence of AVs and SAVs with DRS and road-pricing policies. Does not specify whether fleet is conventional, hybrid, or electric[a]	• The cost effectiveness of traveling with strangers overcomes inconvenience and privacy issues at moderate-to-low fare levels • A moderate fleet size (with one SAV for every 25 people) could encourage a high rate of DRS • When fares for DRS are provided at a 75% discount compared to reference fare levels, a moderate fleet can serve 30% of all trips made during the day, with an average vehicle occupance of 1.48 and a 4.5% increase in VMT • With road-pricing enforced in peak periods, VMT is moderated by 2% for the above fleet

[a]Does not specify whether fleet is conventional, hybrid, or electric.

development could also create higher densities to support additional public transit ridership and allow for the conversion of bus transit to rail transit in urban cores. However, the growth of telecommuting and AVs could also enable longer commutes to become more practical, which could shift consumer preferences in favor of suburban and exurban living. If workers do not have to commute every day, and if those commutes are less expensive and more productive, today's time cost of commuting (and congestion) may be notably reduced. As such, concerns that the introduction of AVs could reduce demand for public transit and encourage increased vehicle use are real. But just as AVs have the potential to reduce driving costs, automated transit vehicles have the opportunity to reduce operating costs and the potential to pass these savings on to riders in the form of lower fares, more frequent service, and better geographic coverage (Shaheen and Cohen, 2018a).

In addition to reducing vehicle ownership, electric SAVs (or SAEVs) have the potential to lower costs and offer flexible public transportation systems. Shaheen et al. (2017) identified potential emerging roles for SAEVs including:

- *Closed Campus*—SAEVs could provide short-distance, point-to-point travel in closed-campus environments that can be easily mapped by software. These locations include: theme parks, resorts, malls, business parks, college campuses, airport terminals, construction sites, downtown centers, real-estate developments, gated communities, industrial centers, and others.
- *First Mile/Last-Mile Connectivity*—Traditionally, public transit has been limited by fixed routes and fixed schedules. Due to these limitations, travelers may find it difficult to complete the first- or last-mile of their journey using public transit. SAEVs may be able to help bridge first- and last-mile gaps in the public transportation network.
- *Low-Density Service*—SAEVs have the potential to provide lower cost and more frequent or responsive public transit options in rural, exurban, and low-density suburban areas where low ridership and high labor costs often contribute to inefficient or cost prohibitive fixed-route service.
- *Off-Peak/Late-Night Service*—Similarly, SAEVs may be able to complement public transit by providing service during off-peak times, especially late at night when service is difficult and costly to provide.
- *Paratransit*—Paratransit services could be provided by SAEVs to meet the needs of people with disabilities; nevertheless, human assistance may still be required.

These applications have the potential to bridge gaps in the transportation network, such as first- and last-mile connections to public transportation, late-night transportation, and service for low-density communities. In the future, SAEVs could have a transformative effect in enhancing equity and accessibility by bridging gaps in the transportation network through the extension of geographic coverage and service availability. However, SAEVs could raise a number of equity concerns, such as the need for a smartphone and/or credit/debit cards to access services and surplus fleets to be stored and charged in low-income neighborhoods.

6. Conclusion

In the coming years, the convergence of automation, electrification, and MOD/MaaS could have a transformative effect on carsharing and its operations, impacts, and business models. These converging innovations could change how carsharing is used and how it interacts with the built environment (e.g., parking, loading, etc.). This convergence also could change the nature of long-standing modal relationships. Although early research suggests that SAEVs could reduce the number of privately owned vehicles and emissions, anecdotal evidence suggests that SAEVs could both serve as a first- and last-mile connection and compete with public transportation. Flexible policymaking is needed to guide SAEV adoption dynamics and to foster sustainable outcomes including: curb management, user incentives, and a variety of pricing mechanisms. Pricing, in particular, could be used to mitigate induced demand that could occur if SAEVs are low cost and convenient enough to encourage additional VMT/VKT. Pricing policies could include: (1) road usage fees that charge users based on distance traveled and (2) congestion pricing that charges vehicles for driving through a particular zone. Pricing can also vary by time of day (to decrease congestion impacts) and occupancy (to encourage sharing). Geospatial and temporal variations, including urban density and public transit service frequency, along with socio-demographics and cultural norms could result in a range of variable impacts. Policymakers should consider establishing a framework to help mitigate the potential negative impacts of automation on public transit ridership, VMT/VKT, social equity, and land use.

The convergence of automation, electrification and MOD/MaaS has the potential to act as a "multimodal multiplier," supporting a larger pool of travelers and modal options through a "network effect." This could improve the efficiency, effectiveness, and quality of multimodal trips by connecting public transportation with carsharing and other mobility strategies. At present, curbs and sidewalks are being disrupted by the growing array of shared-mobility services in urban environments. In the future, cities will continue to face competition for access to their rights-of-way. As carsharing evolves toward automation, policies that encourage transportation equity for underserved communities and vehicle sharing (both pooled and sequential) should be explored. To address the ongoing evolution of shared mobility, more research and policy understanding are needed to maximize its social and environmental benefits.

Acknowledgments

The authors would like to thank the American Planning Association, the California Department of Transportation (Caltrans), the Mineta Transportation Institute, and the U.S. Department of Transportation for their generous support of this work. Special thanks to the Carsharing Association, carsharing and shared mobility operators, industry experts, and policymakers who make this research possible. The contents of this chapter reflect the views of the authors and do not necessarily indicate sponsor acceptance.

References

6t, 2014. One-Way Carsharing: Which Alternative to Private Cars?. Available at https://www.6-t.co/wp-content/uploads/2014/05/AD_ExecutiveSummary_140708-copie-2.pdf.

Becker, H., Ciari, F., Axhausen, K.W., 2018. Measuring the car ownership impact of free-floating car-sharing–a case study in Basel, Switzerland. Transp. Res. Part D: Transp. Environ. 65, 51–62.

Biondi, E., Boldrini, C., Bruno, R., 2016. The impact of regulated electric fleets on the power grid: the car sharing case. In: Research and Technologies for Society and Industry Leveraging a Better Tomorrow (RTSI), 2016 IEEE 2nd International Forum on on Research and Technologies for Society and Industry Leveraging a Better Tomorrow (RTSI) 2016 Sep 7. IEEE, pp. 1–6.

Cervero, R., 2003. City CarShare: first-year travel demand impacts. Transp. Res. Rec. 1839 (1), 159–166.

Cervero, R., Tsai, Y., 2004. City CarShare in San Francisco: second-year travel demand and car ownership impacts. Transp. Res. Rec. 1887, 117–127.

Cervero, R., Golub, A., Nee, B., 2007. City CarShare: longer-term travel demand and car ownership impacts. Transp. Res. Rec. 1992 (1), 70–80.

Chen, T.D., Kockelman, K.M., Hanna, J.P., 2016. Operations of a shared, autonomous, electric vehicle fleet: implications of vehicle & charging infrastructure decisions. Transp. Res. A Policy Pract. 94, 243–254.

Chow, J., 2018. Dual Rebalancing Strategies for Electric Vehicle Carsharing Operations. C2SMART. Available from, http://c2smart.engineering.nyu.edu/2018/05/11/dual-rebalancing-strategies-for-electric-vehicle-carsharing-operations/#1518033148087-355212d9-bd9e2670-5054.

Cohen, A., Shaheen, S., 2016. Planning for Shared Mobility. The American Planning Association, Chicago. Available at https://www.planning.org/publications/report/9107556/.

Communauto, 2000. Potentiel de L'Auto-Partage Dans Le Cadre d'Une Politique de Gestion de La Demande en Transport. In: Forum de L'AQTR, Gaz à Effet de Serre: Transport et Développement, Kyoto: Une Opportunité d'Affaires? Montréal, Canada. February 7. Available at https://docplayer.fr/403714-L-auto-partage-et-le-transport-en-commun.html.

Cooper, G., Howes, D., Mye, P., 2000. The Missing Link: An Evaluation of CarSharing Portland Inc., Portland, Oregon. State of Oregon Department of Environmental Quality, Portland, OR.

Dill, J., Howland, S., McNeil, N., 2014. Peer-to-Peer Carsharing: A Preliminary Analysis of Vehicle Owners in Portland, Oregon, and the Potential to Meet Policy Objectives. Transportation Research Board Annual Meeting, Washington D.C., pp. 1–22.

Eckhouse, B., Stringer, D., Hodges, J., 2019. The World Still Doesn't Have Enough Places to Plug in Cars. Bloomberg.

Fagnant, D.J., Kockelman, K.M., 2018. Dynamic ride-sharing and fleet sizing for a system of shared autonomous vehicles in Austin, Texas. Transportation 45 (1), 143–158.

Firnkorn, J., Müller, M., 2011. What will be the environmental effects of new free-floating car-sharing systems? The case of car2go in Ulm. Ecol. Econ. 70 (8), 1519–1528.

Fraiberger, S., Sundararajan, A., 2015. Peer-to-peer rental markets in the sharing economy. In: NYU Stern School of Business Research Paper. Available at: http://ssrn.com/abstract=2574337.

Frost & Sullivan, 2018. Global Electric Vehicle Market Outlook. Frost & Sullivan. [Internet]; 2018 Mar 27 [cited 2019 Jan 4]. Available from, http://www.frost.com/sublib/display-report.do?id=MDAB-01-00-00-00&bdata=bnVsbEB%2BQEJhY2tAfkAxNTQ2NjI4NjEyMTUz.

Galinsky, E., 2016. Flexiblity: Central to an Effective Workplace. Retrieved from SHRM: https://www.shrm.org/hr-today/trends-and-forecasting/special-reports-and-expert-views/pages/ellen-galinsky.aspx.

Giesel, F., Nobis, C., 2016. The impact of carsharing on car ownership in German cities. Transp. Res. Procedia 19, 215–224.

Gleave, S.D., 2017. Caplus Annual Survey of Car Clubs 2016/2017. Tech Rep, Leeds.

Greenblatt, J.B., Saxena, S., 2015. Autonomous taxis could greatly reduce greenhouse-gas emissions of US light-duty vehicles. Nat. Clim. Chang. 5 (9), 860.

Gurumurthy, K.M., Kockelman, K.M., Simoni, M.D., 2019. Benefits and costs of ride-sharing in shared automated vehicles across Austin, Texas: opportunities for congestion pricing. Transp. Res. Rec. 2673, 0361198119850785.

Hertzke, P., Müller, N., Schenk, S., 2018. The Global Electric-Vehicle Market is Amped Up and on the Rise [Internet]. McKinsey&Company. 2018 May. Available from, https://www.mckinsey.com/industries/automotive-and-assembly/our-insights/the-global-electric-vehicle-market-is-amped-up-and-on-the-rise.

Holder, M., 2019. BP Teams Up With DiDi to Develop China's EV Charging Network [Internet]. Business Green. https://www.businessgreen.com/bg/news/3079992/bp-teams-up-with-didi-to-develop-ev-charging-network-across-china. accessed 8.16.19.

Jensen, N., 2001. The Co-Operative Auto Network Social and Environmental Report, 2000–2001. Cooperative Auto Network, Vancouver, British Columbia.

Kane, M., 2018. Shell Begins Rollout Of Ultra-Fast Chargers In Europe [Internet]. Shell Begins Roll. Ultra-Fast Charg. Eur. https://insideevs.com/news/340683/shell-begins-rollout-of-ultra-fast-chargers-in-europe/. (accessed 8.16.19).

Katzev, R., 1999. CarSharing Portland: Review and Analysis of Its First Year. Elsevier, pp. 1–87.

Koettl, J., 2016. Boundless Life Expectancy: The Future of Aging Populations. The Brookings Institution, Washington D.C. Retrieved from The Brookings Institution.
Kolko, J., 2017. Seattle Climbs but Austin Sprawls: The Myth of the Return to Cities. Retrieved from The New York Times, https://www.nytimes.com/2017/05/22/upshot/seattle-climbs-but-austin-sprawls-the-myth-of-the-return-to-cities.html.
Kummer, F., 2019. Wawa Plans to Double Number of its Tesla Super-Charging Stations [Internet]. The Philadelphia Inquirer. https://www.inquirer.com/science/climate/wawa-electric-vehicle-charging-stations-tesla-20190807.html. accessed 8.16.19.
Lane, C., 2005. PhillyCarShare: first-year social and mobility impacts of carsharing in Philadelphia, Pennsylvania. Transp. Res. Rec. 1927, 158–166.
Le Vine, S., Polak, J., 2017. The impact of free-floating carsharing on car ownership: early-stage findings from London. Transp. Policy 75, 119–127.
Lichtenberg, D.S.J., Hanel, F., 2007. Carsharing und ÖPNV: Nutzen für beide? Der Nahverkehr 25 (11), 37–41.
Martin, E., Shaheen, S., 2011a. The impact of carsharing on public transit and non-motorized travel: an exploration of north American carsharing survey data. Energies 4, 2094–2114.
Martin, E., Shaheen, S., 2011b. Greenhouse gas emission impacts of carsharing in North America. IEEE Trans. Intell. Transp. Syst. 12 (4), 1074–1086.
Martin, E., Shaheen, S., 2016. Impacts of car2go on Vehicle Ownership, Modal Shift, Vehicle Miles Traveled, and Greenhouse Gas Emissions: An Analysis of Five North American Cities. Transportation Sustainability Research Center, Berkeley, CA. Available at http://innovativemobility.org/wp-content/uploads/2016/07/Impactsofcar2go_FiveCities_2016.pdf.
Martin, E., Shaheen, S., Lidicker, J., 2010. Impact of carsharing on household vehicle holdings. Transp. Res. Rec. 2143, 150–158.
McPhee, D., 2019. BP Starts UK Rollout of 400 Ultra-Fast EV Charge-Points [Internet]. Energy Voice. https://www.energyvoice.com/otherenergy/205615/bp-starts-uk-rollout-of-400-ultra-fast-ev-charge-points/. accessed 8.16.19.
Millard-Ball, A., Murray, G., ter Schure, J., Fox, C., Burkhardt, J., 2005. Car-Sharing: Where and How it Succeeds. vol. 108. Transportation Research Board.
Namazu, M., Dowlatabadi, H., 2018. Vehicle ownership reduction: a comparison of one-way and two-way carsharing systems. Transp. Policy 64, 38–50.
Nicholas, M., Hall, D., 2018. Lessons Learned on Early Electric Vehicle Fast-Charging Deployments. The International Council on Clean Transportation, Washington, DC.
Norwegian Electric Vehicle Association, 2019. Norway Reaches Historical Electric Car Market Share [Internet]. Retrieved from: https://elbil.no/norway-reaches-historic-electric-car-market-share/.
Nourinejad, M., Zhu, S., Bahrami, S., Roorda, M.J., 2015. Vehicle relocation and staff rebalancing in one-way carsharing systems. Transport Res. E-Log 1 (81), 98–113.
Office of Highway Policy Information, 2018. Average Annual Miles per Driver by Age Group [Internet]. Federal Highway Administration. 2018 March, https://www.fhwa.dot.gov/ohim/onh00/bar8.htm.
Plungis, J., 2019. How the Electric Car Charging Network Is Expanding [Internet]. Consumer Reports. https://www.consumerreports.org/hybrids-evs/electric-car-charging-network-is-expanding/. accessed 8.16.19.
Price, J., Hamilton, C., 2005. Arlington pilot carshare program. In: First-Year Report. Available at http://mobilitylab.org/wp-content/uploads/2012/02/ArlingtonCarshareProgram.pdf.
Price, J., DeMaio, P., Hamilton, C., 2006. Arlington Pilot Carshare Program: 2006 Report. Available at https://mobilitylab.org/research-document/2006-arlington-county-carshare-program-study/.

Reagan, C., Picker, L., 2017. It's More Than Amazon: Why Retail is in Distress Now. Retrieved from CNBC, https://www.cnbc.com/2017/05/05/its-more-than-amazon-why-retail-is-in-distress-now.html.
Rydén, C., Morin, E., 2005. Mobility services for urban sustainability. In: Environmental Assessment. Report WP 6. Trivector Traffic AB, Stockhom, Sweden. 213.170.188.3/moses/Downloads/reports/del_6.pdf.
Shaheen, S., Cohen, A., 2007. Worldwide carsharing growth: an international comparison. Transp. Res. Rec. 1992, 81–89.
Shaheen, S., Cohen, A., 2018a. Is it time for a public transit renaissance?: navigating travel behavior, technology, and business model shifts in a brave new world. J. Public Transp. 21 (1), 8.
Shaheen, S., Cohen, A., 2018b. Mobility on Demand: Three Key Components [Internet]. Retrieved from Move Forward, https://www.move-forward.com/mobility-on-demand-three-key-components/.
Shaheen, S., Stocker, A., 2015. Information Brief: Carsharing for Business, Zipcar Case Study & Impact Analysis. Available at http://innovativemobility.org/wp-content/uploads/2015/07/Zipcar_Corporate_Final_v6.pdf.
Shaheen, S., Cohen, A., Roberts, D., 2006. Carsharing in North America: market growth, current developments, and future potential. Transp. Res. Rec. 1986, 116–124.
Shaheen, S., Mallery, M., Kingsley, K., 2012. Personal vehicle sharing services in North America. Res. Transp. Bus. Manag. 3, 71–81.
Shaheen, S., Cohen, A., Yelchuru, B., Sarkhili, S., 2017. Mobility on Demand Operational Concept Report. U.S. Department of Transportation, Washington D.C.
Shaheen, S., Cohen, A., Jaffee, M., 2018a. Innovative Mobility Carsharing Outlook. Transportation Sustainability Research Center, University of California, Berkeley. Spring 2018.
Shaheen, S., Cohen, A., Jaffee, M., 2018b. Innovative Mobility Carsharing Outlook. Transportation Sustainability Research Center, University of California, Berkeley. Winter 2018.
Shaheen, S., Martin, E., Bansal, A., 2018c. Peer-To-Peer (P2P) Carsharing: Understanding Early Markets, Social Dynamics, and Behavioral Impacts. Transportation Sustainability Research Center, Berkeley. Available at https://cloudfront.escholarship.org/dist/prd/content/qt7s8207tb/qt7s8207tb.pdf?t=p6n4ys&v=lg.
Shaheen, S., Martin, E., Bansal, A., 2018d. One-Way Electric Vehicle Carsharing in San Diego: An Exploration of the Behavioral Impacts of Pricing Incentives on Operational Efficiency. Transportation Sustainability Research Center, Berkeley. Available at: https://cloudfront.escholarship.org/dist/prd/content/qt25x091bh/qt25x091bh.pdf?t=pp3e7k&v=lg.
Sochor, J., Arby, H., Karlsson, M., Sarasini, S., 2016. A topological approach to mobility as a service: a proposed tool for understanding requirements and effects, and for aiding the integration of societal goals. Res. Transp. Bus. Manag. 27, 3–14.
Stocker, A., Lazarus, J., Becker, S., Shaheen, S., 2016. North American College/University Market Carsharing Impacts: Results from Zipcar's College Travel Study 2015. Transportation Sustainability Research Center, Berkeley.
Stockholm, City of (Sweden), 2005. Mobility Services for Urban Sustainability: Environmental Assessment. Report WP 6. Prepared by Christian Ryden and and Emma Morin, Trivector.
Swigonski, F., 2017. Car sharing, Electrification, and Automation are Converging into a New Mobility System. Advanced Energy Economy. Available at: https://blog.aee.net/car-sharing-electrification-and-automation-are-converging-into-a-new-mobility-system.

Walb, C., Loudon, W., 1986. Evaluation of the short-term auto rental (Star) in San Francisco, CA. In: Final Report (No. UMTA-CA-06-0166-86-1).
Zhao, D., Li, X., Zhang, Y., 2018. Electric Vehicle Sharing Planning and Operations, Center for Transportation, Environment, and Community Health. February 1. Available from, https://cpb-usw2.wpmucdn.com/sites.coecis.cornell.edu/dist/6/132/files/2017/11/USF_YR1_LI-ZHANG_FINAL_ELECTRICAL-VEHICLE-SHARING-2hi9qf1.pdf.
Zipcar, 2005a. Zipcar Customer Survey Shows Car-Sharing Leads to Car Shedding. Available at https://www.autorentalnews.com/75124/zipcar-releases-survey-on-car-sharing-impact.
Zipcar, 2005b. Zipcar Customer Survey Shows Car-Sharing Leads to Car Shedding [Internet]. Retrieved fromhttp://www.zipcar.com/press/releases/press-2.

CHAPTER SIX

Bike share

Elliot Fishman*, Vaughn Allan
Institute for Sensible Transport, Melbourne, Australia
*Corresponding author: e-mail address: info@sensibletransport.org.au

Contents

Abstract

This chapter reviews the literature covering the burgeoning topic of bike share. Few transport modes have expanded as rapidly as bike share in the 21st century. From little more than a handful of systems 15 years ago, there are now well over 4.5 million bikes in the global bike share fleet, operating in over 1500 cities. The health, space efficiency and environmental benefits of cycling, coupled with technological developments

Advances in Transport Policy and Planning, Volume 4
ISSN 2543-0009
https://doi.org/10.1016/bs.atpp.2019.05.003

that have underpinned shared mobility platforms helps to explain this unprecedented growth and interest in bike share. Bike share is now seen as one part of the "mobility as a service" package that can help to provide transport options without being encumbered with vehicle ownership the negative impacts associated with widespread car use. This chapter concludes that in order to continue bike share's role in helping to make cities more liveable and sustainable, cities need to place greater attention on creating bicycle friendly streetscapes and discourage the widespread use of the car for short car trips in cities around the world.

Keywords: Shared transport, Bike share, Sustainable mobility, Cycling, Mobility as a service

1. Introduction

Few modes of transport have experienced the rapid growth experienced in bike share. There are now well over 4.5 million bikes included in the global bike share fleet, operating in well over 1500 cities. This chapter reviews the growing body of work on a wide range of sub-topics within this growing field. Bike share is inextricably linked with the emergence of the sharing economy generally. What was once a relatively stagnant set of transport choices in cities has now seen a widening of options that include App based ride sourcing platforms (e.g., Uber, Didi), peer-2-peer car share (e.g., Snappcar, Getaround, CarNextDoor), and on demand App based public transport. To a greater or lesser extent, these non-traditional forms of transport have diversified mobility options in cities, which has the potential to reduce car ownership and use (Shaheen and Cohen, 2018). These developments are now categorized as *Mobility as a Service* (MaaS) and also include the burgeoning shared e-scooter sector,[a] which has rapidly developed in North America, Western Europe and Australasia during the 2017–19 period, with many other markets beginning to see e-scooters emerge as an additional transport option. While interesting, e-scooters have not yet been operating long enough for a sufficient body of research to develop and are therefore not included in this review. As will be discussed, the 2018 acquisition of the bike share company *JUMP* (formally *SocialBicycles*) by the dominant ride sourcing service, *Uber*, signifies a shift toward a "*one App, access-all-modes*" platform that appears to be the "end game" for many of the competing MaaS companies.

[a] E-scooters are not the focus of this chapter as they do not have pedals and therefore not considered a bicycle.

1.1 The bicycle's place in the new urban mobility agenda

While the dependence people have on the automobile in many cities is widespread and long standing, there are signs that this dependence has begun to weaken over the last decade (Van Dender and Clever, 2013). There are a variety of complex reasons for this (see Goodwin and Van Dender, 2013) and while it is too early to know precisely which factors are causing this global, somewhat slow shift away from car use in some countries, the trend is surprisingly widespread among developed countries (Van Dender and Clever, 2013). A combination of changing attitudes, demographics, lifestyle preferences, and technology are cited as contributing factors to the shift away from automobile dependent lifestyles (Hoffmann et al., 2015). A growing awareness of the importance of *liveability* has led to an emerging recalibration of city life, in which the car's long held position as the centerpiece of people's mobility options is beginning to change (Stapleton et al., 2017).

The bicycle, owing to its positive impact on physical activity, air quality, and climate change combined with its space efficiency and affordability has emerged as a critical element of this new urban mobility (Giles-Corti et al., 2016; Sallis et al., 2016; Stevenson et al., 2016). Fig. 1 demonstrates

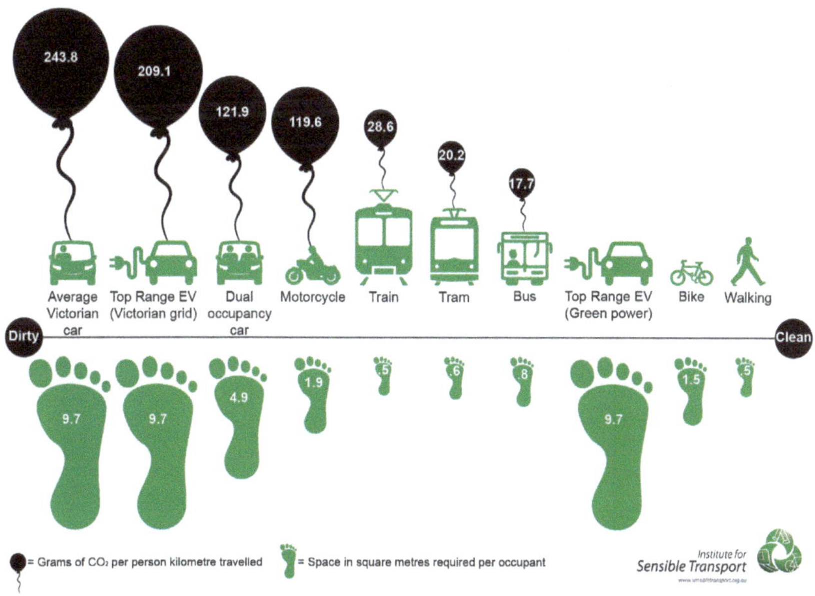

Fig. 1 Emissions and space efficient—different modes. *Source: Davies, L., Fishman, E., 2018. Transport Strategy Refresh: Transport, Greenhouse Gas Emissions and Air Quality. Melbourne: Institute for Sensible Transport, commissioned by the City of Melbourne.*

the greenhouse gas intensity of different transport modes (represented by black balloons) and the space consumption (illustrated with the footprints). This demonstrates that the bicycle, owning to its small environmental and space footprint is well suited to cities seeking to minimize their congestion and environmental issues.

As Ivan Illich notes only the bicycle really allows people to go from door to door without walking (1973, p. 62) and it is this unique attribute that has helped to refocus the attention of city and transport planners to the role the bicycle is able to play in urban areas. Ultimately of course, it cannot and should not be "*about the bike*," but rather on the benefits the bicycle brings to cities, in the form of carbon free, healthy, low cost and space efficient mobility. As more cities begin to recognize the benefits cycling offers, bike share has become an increasingly popular method of enhancing transport choice, urban productivity and sustainability (Buehler and Pucher, 2020).

1.2 Bike share in the context of transport systems

One useful method of thinking about bike share (and other modes of transport for that matter) is by isolating the three fundamental elements that each mode of transport relies upon. Professor Donald Shoup, best known for his work on parking policy, has identified that each mode of transport consists of three elements, as shown in Fig. 2.

Each mode of transport typically requires the above three elements (with the exception of walking). Maritime transport, for example, requires ships

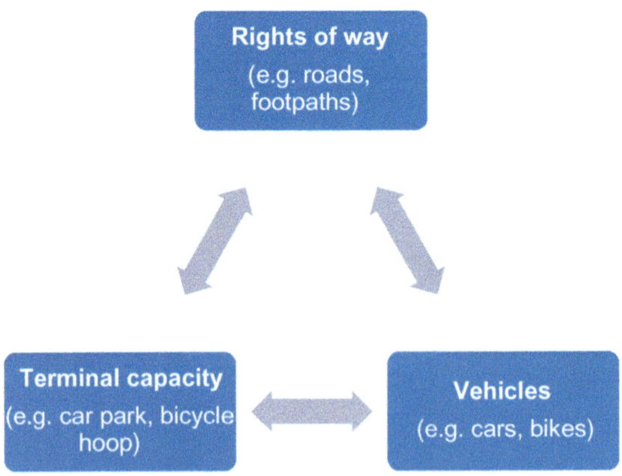

Fig. 2 Transport mode—three elements. *Source: Shoup, D., 2010. The high cost of free parking: Key note address.* In: *Fishman, E. (ed.)* The High Cost of Free Parking Seminar. *Melbourne Town Hall: Institute for Sensible Transport.*

(the vehicle), shipping lanes (rights of way) and ports (terminal capacity). For bicycling, the vehicles are bicycles, the rights of way are streets and bicycle paths, and terminal capacity are bicycle racks or similar devices to lock bicycles. "Traditional" bike share programs address two of these three elements, namely, they provide the *vehicle* (bicycle) and the *terminal capacity* (docking station). Dockless bike share only provides the *vehicle*, with city governments required to provide the *terminal capacity* (bicycle parking), in addition to sufficient rights of way (bike lanes and paths). Failing to provide sufficient rights of way (e.g., protected bicycle lanes) can act as a barrier to bike share use.

Importantly, bike share is seen as a first mile/last mile solution (Shaheen et al., 2010), helping to improve access to and from public transport (Parkes et al., 2013). The integration of cycling and public transport is said to make up for the weakness of both. The Netherlands provides a good example of what can be achieved when the bicycle network is planned to complement the rail system (Martens, 2004). Kager et al. (2016) argue that when planned to complement each other, the bicycle is able to "soften" the rigidity of the public transport system, and enhance land use and transport planning outcomes. In the Netherlands, around 49% of train journeys can start with a bicycle trip (Ministerie van Verkeer en Waterstaat, 2009). A bike share network designed to act as a feeder to public transport can substantially enhance the functional catchment of public transport. Why is this important for bike share? Bike share, by allowing for one-way bicycle trips, can be used to connect people to transport hubs, allowing them to make their onward journey while leaving the bicycle at the station, available for another rider. Fig. 3, taken outside one of Beijing's metro stations, is a good demonstration of the public's willingness to combine bike share with public transport, a theme that is consistent across bike share programs in North America (LDA Consulting, 2017; Kaufman et al., 2015), London (Transport for London, 2018), and Australia (Lansell, 2011). Fig. 3 also demonstrates why dockless bike share has been controversial, as large numbers of bicycles parked on footpaths can reduce accessibility for pedestrians and wheelchair users.

This chapter reviews key findings and themes to emerge from the growing body of literature on bike share, including the impacts these programs are having on cities, emerging tech trends and key factors in the success of bike share.

2. A brief history of bike share

Bike share has had a checkered history in the half century since the first "program," known as *Witte Fietsen* ("White Bikes" in Dutch) was launched

Fig. 3 Dockless bike share parked outside a Beijing Metro Station. *Image: Institute for Sensible Transport.*

Fig. 4 White Bike program, Amsterdam mid-1960s. *Image: Luud Schimmelpennink.*

on the streets of Amsterdam in 1965 (Fig. 4). Although frequently referred to as the first bike share program, it was in fact little more than a political stunt by the prominent activist group Provo (as in to provoke). Witte Fietsen consisted of 5–10 bicycles, hand painted white, and left on the street for people to use freely (Schimmelpennink, 2014). The total absence of any security mechanisms led to theft and vandalism, and the rapid demise of the "program" (DeMaio, 2009).

While Witte Fietsen was short lived, the concept of bike share had been born. The theft and vandalism that led to the demise of Witte Fietsen meant that bike share made little progress in the years immediately following Amsterdam's experiment. It was not until technological advancements enabled affordable security mechanisms to be added to the bicycles that other cities began to successfully embark on bike share programs of their own.

The first city to offer a government authorized bike share scheme was La Rochelle in France, in 1976. Consisting of 250 bicycles, the system was low tech and each bicycle was taken off the street at the end of the day, and replaced again in the morning. Interestingly, rather than a door-to-door form of transport, the bike share program was initially conceived as a kind of "park and ride" initiative in an attempt to encourage motorists to park on the outskirts of the city and make the final leg of the journey on the "*auto-velos*" as the bikes were originally called, meaning car-bikes (Hure and Passalacqua, 2017). The bikes were intended to be free for everyone to use, and in fact were inspired by the shopping trolley; in that they were available to be freely shared between people according to need.

3. The evolution and growth of bike share

Some researchers have categorized the evolution of bike share systems into four "generations" (Parkes et al., 2013). White Bikes described above is known as a first-generation bike share "system," characterized by no payment or security functions. Second-generation programs involved a coin deposit system (similar to trolleys at a supermarket or airport). The first large-scale second-generation program launched in Copenhagen in 1995, but the anonymity also exposed the system to theft/vandalism (DeMaio, 2009). The evolution of bike share is captured in Fig. 5. This chapter treats dockless bike share as fourth generation.

The problems experienced by these first two generations of bike share led to the development of third-generation systems, which are characterized by dedicated docking stations (in which bicycles are picked up and returned), as well as automated credit card payment and other technologies to allow the tracking of the bicycles (Shaheen et al., 2013).

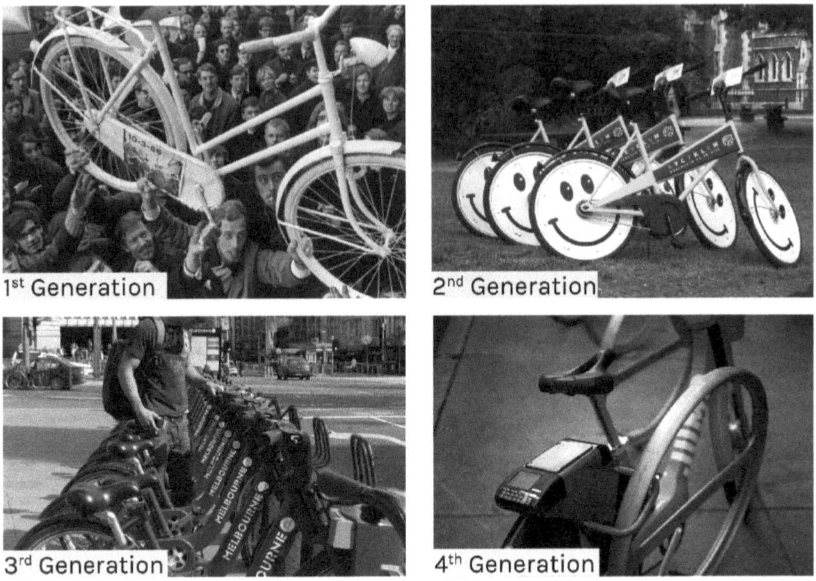

Fig. 5 The evolution of bike share. *Source: Fishman, E., 2019.* Bike Share, *Routledge.*

It is these elements, in combination with growing public policy interest in cycling (Buehler and Pucher, 2020) that have enabled the rapid growth of bike share programs globally (Fishman, 2015). Up until 2016, almost all of the bike share programs established since 2005 could be classed as third-generation. The features of fourth-generation systems are not quite so clear, but are said to include dockless systems, easier installation, electric assistance and transit smartcard integration (Parkes et al., 2013).

The bike share sector is currently in a state of flux; new technologies and business models have caused city governments to re-think public investment in bike share. As of early-2019, the commercial sector continues to demonstrate an enthusiasm for launching and managing bike share services without public subsidy. As to how this might influence the evolution of bike share is unclear. One of the trends evident in many North American cities, as well as growing number of cities around the globe is the emergence of e-scooters and it is uncertain what impact the growth of e-scooters may have on bike share evolution. Some cities, such as Brisbane, Australia have (paradoxically) had their highest bike share usage in the month e-scooters launched, while other cities have seen e-scooters cannibalize bike share usage. As tech companies and traditional vehicle manufacturers merge and acquire bike share firms, how bike share may evolve in the next decade is difficult to determine.

3.1 Bike share's growth

In the past decade, the number of cities operating bike share programs has increased from 13 in 2004 to over 1500 cities as of 2019. There are now over 2130 individual bike share programs, with many cities having multiple bike share programs (Meddin, 2018). As shown in Fig. 6, the global growth in bike share began around 2005–07. It was during this period that two French cities launched relatively large schemes that used street advertising contracts as a method of paying for bike share. Lyon and Paris launched their bike share programs in 2005 and 2007, respectively, and Paris in particular attracted a great deal of public attention, owing to both its status as an international city, and the sheer size of the program (~20,000 bikes). Many Mayors and other city officials from around the globe traveled to Paris and decided their city too should have a bike share program. In this sense, Paris became the catalyst for bike share's rapid global growth.

The rise of dockless bike share has accounted for much of the growth beginning in 2015 (Meddin and DeMaio, 2016). As of January 2019, it is estimated there are now over 20 million bike share bikes, with the overwhelming majority of them being dockless. It is now increasingly difficult to determine the number of bicycles within bike sharing systems, as there are multiple commercial suppliers placing bicycles in the same city, competing with one another, often without any formal government involvement. This was certainly the case in the 2015–17 period and this coupled with the myriad of

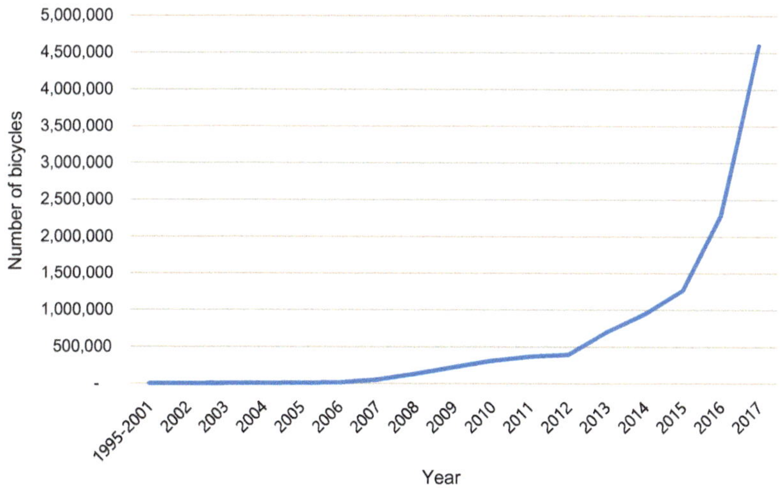

Fig. 6 Bike share fleet, global estimate. *Source: Russell Meddin.*

issues associated with dockless bike share have prompted city governments to begin regulating prospective operators (Yanocha, 2018).

The United States, a relative latecomer to bike share, has seen a rapid increase in the number of cities offering bike share. It is estimated that the total number of bike share bikes in the United States rose from 42,500 by the end of 2016, to around 100,000 just 12 months later, with ridership growing by 25% (NACTO, 2018). In 2016 it was estimated riders took over 28 million trips using bike share in the United States (Institute for Transportation and Development Policy, 2018). Several cities now include a combination of docked and dockless bike share in the United States (e.g., San Francisco and Washington, DC.). While dockless bike share has clearly grown more rapidly than the docked systems, some research from the United States suggests that docked bike share has a higher level of use (in terms of trips per day per bike). For instance, the NACTO found that while dockless bikes accounted for 44% of all bike share bicycles, they make up only 4% of all trips (NACTO, 2018).

Bike share is not restricted to wealthy countries/cities, and in fact, most of the world's bike share bikes are located in developing countries. China in particular stands out, with a large number of cities successfully integrating bike share, docked or dockless, into their transport system. Dockless in particular has fuelled the growth of bike share in many parts of the world. While the largest of these systems are in China, South America has seen the introduction of bike schemes with over 1000 bicycles in Santiago, Chile, and Buenos Aires, Argentina, to name just two. Mexico City also has a well-used system with over 6000 bikes and Guadalajara has a system of almost 2000 bikes. A handful of Indian cities have small scale bike share programs, with Pune currently accommodating 3000 dockless bikes, making it the largest system in India (Meddin, 2018).

4. Dockless bike share and its challenges

The rise of dockless bike share caught many cities by surprise and most have found themselves having to create or update regulations in order to address some of the issues associated with their emergence in cities (Yanocha, 2018). Unlike docked bike share, dockless system very often are introduced by the private sector without government support. The introduction of these "floating" systems present opportunities for large scale bike share without the level of government expenditure required for some docked bike share systems (Institute for Transportation and Development

Policy, 2018). The lack of docking locations can, however, lead to haphazard parking and public nuisance issues (Fishman, 2019).

In mid-2017, due to the rapid advancement of dockless bike share systems in hundreds of cities across the globe, a study was commissioned on the parking related issues associated with dockless bike share (see Fishman, 2017). In the 24 months since this investigation was undertaken, a number of dockless bike share firms have since abandoned the market. For instance, of the five companies operating dockless bike share in Sydney, Australia, only one continues to operate (Mobike), and at a much smaller scale than when entering the market. A number of cities, including Beijing, have seen a retraction in the scale of dockless bike share operations, due primarily to government and public concerns regarding the space consumed by masses of parked (and sometimes discarded bikes). This study found that a lack of engagement with government agencies led to a haphazard arrangement for parking bicycles and little in the way of asset management protocol when bicycles were parked in a manner that blocked public access or methods of retrieving damaged bicycles. The bicycles were also found to be of poor quality, with many in an unrideable condition and kick stands that failed to maintain the bike in an upright position in strong winds.

To address the issues associated with the emergence of dockless bike share bikes, it was suggested a regulatory framework be developed, similar to what Seattle, San Francisco and a number of other U.S. cities have begun to develop. This provides a transparent framework that makes the rights and responsibilities of all parties clearer, and reduces the risk of dockless bikes reducing the amenity of the public realm. A number of researchers have identified that in order for dockless bike share to achieve their potential, it will be necessary to provide sufficient opportunities to park them safely and conveniently (Fuller et al., 2018).

Finally, the degree to which the public and the media view dockless bike share as a *public nuisance* rather than *public service* is very much related to how much it is used. In some cities, it can be common for dockless bikes to sit idle for days, or even weeks, without attracting any riders (e.g., Melbourne, Australia's experience with *oBike*). This serves to reinforce a public perception that these bicycles are a public nuisance, not serving a public need. Fig. 7 offers a conceptual model illustrating the relationship between public acceptance and usage.

As usage rises, so too does public acceptance (because the value to the community is evident). This model was developed after the author observed that the cities with well used dockless bike share programs do not appear to attract the level of public criticism of low usage programs (Fishman, 2017).

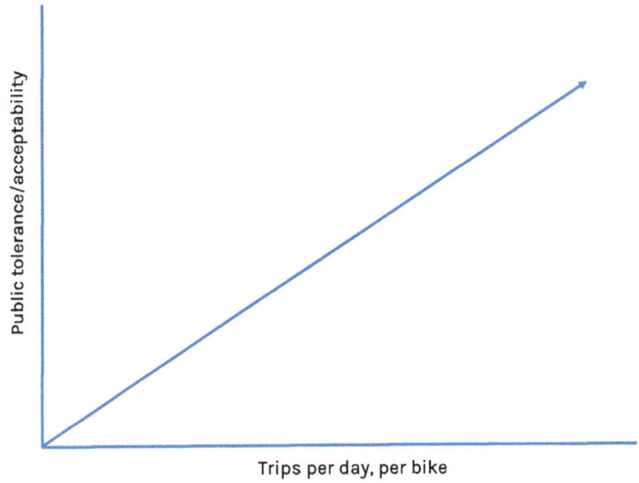

Fig. 7 Dockless bike share acceptability and use—a conceptual model. *Source: Fishman, E., 2017. Bike Share Parking Infrastructure Guidelines. Melbourne: Prepared by the Institute for Sensible Transport for VicRoads.*

Conversely, low usage docked bike share systems do not attract the same level of public criticism, theft, and vandalism compared to their dockless cousins. A key reason for this difference is the asserted rights to space within the urban environment. Docking stations signal to the public that share bikes *belong* within the space afforded by the station. Because the public expect to find share bikes at that location and all the bikes look the same, it is impossible to tell whether the bikes are been used a little or a lot. Dockless bikes, on the other hand, are rarely afforded any rights to public space. The idleness of an individual dockless share bike is obvious without a designated parking location. This leaves dockless bikes as "*matter out of place*" within the public realm and open to criticism when bikes have been left unused for a period of time. Providing bike share systems, including dockless varieties, rights to the city is essential to improving its usage and standing with the general public.

The implication of this relationship for cities with dockless bike share, or planning to implement it, is that everything must be done to maximize its use. While an effective agreement with bike share providers is critical, cities themselves need to ensure their bicycle infrastructure network encourages cycling. In most cases, this will mean substantial investments in protected bicycle lanes, off road cycling connections, designated parking areas, and measures that boost the competitive advantage of bike share over private car use for short to medium distance inner city journeys.

5. Impacts of bike share

As highlighted in the introduction, bike share has become attractive due to the benefits they offer cities seeking to increase liveability and sustainability outcomes. Understanding the impacts of bike share is critical to their future role in cities and can help determine whether public investment is warranted in their expansion. The degree to which bike share is able to positively impact on cities is dependent on the influence these programs have on transport mode choice (Médard de Chardon et al., 2017, Fishman, 2019) and the bikes' level of use. Bike share programs that successfully transfer trips formally done by car and are heavily used will have a greater impact than programs that are seldom used and rarely replace car trips. Added to these benefits are potential travel time savings, increased transport mode flexibility and enhanced possibilities for integration with public transport (Fishman, 2015, Shaheen et al., 2010). There may also be some benefit when bike share transfers peak hour public transport journeys, as one seat freed up on a heavily loaded train is in essence a new seat made available for someone else (Fishman, 2015; Shaheen et al., 2012a).

Fig. 8 offers an illustration of the number of trips per day, on a per bike basis, for a selection of cities for which data was available. It shows bike use varies widely, from almost 6 trips per day, per bike (Lyon), to as low as 0.3 trips per day, per bike (Brisbane). The reasons explaining the difference in ridership levels is explored comprehensively in Fishman (2019).

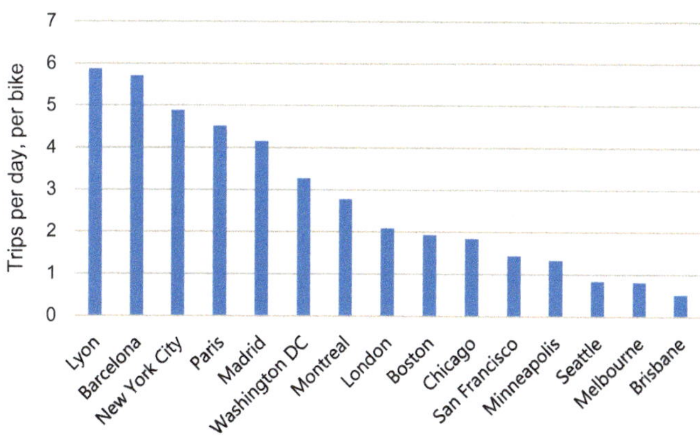

Fig. 8 Bike share ridership, selected cities (2015). *Source: Fishman, E., 2019.* Bike Share, *Routledge.*

5.1 Impacts on car use

As highlighted earlier, many of the benefits people associate with bike share are dependent on the degree to which it acts as a substitute for car use (e.g., greenhouse gas emissions, congestion). Médard de Chardon et al. have described that when bike share typically replaces pedestrian or public transport journeys, the benefits of bike share are diminished (Médard de Chardon et al., 2017).

An increasingly common question directed toward bike share users is "For your last bike share trip, what mode of transport would you have used if bike share was not available?" The answer to this question is crucial to developing an understanding of the impact bike share has on transport sustainability and many of the other benefits of bike share identified above. A consistent theme has emerged when examining responses to this question; *most of the trips are replacing trips formerly made by public transport and walking* (Fishman et al., 2014a). The results for a selected number of bike share cities are provided in Fig. 9.

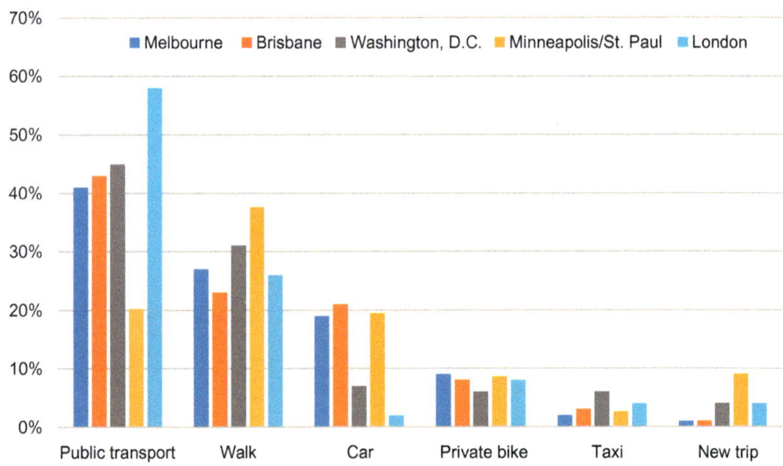

Fig. 9 Mode being substituted by bike share, selected cities. *Source: Melbourne and Brisbane (Fishman, E., Washington, S., Haworth, N., 2014a. Bike share's impact on car use: evidence from the United States, great Britain, and Australia. Transp. Res. Part D: Transp. Environ. 31, 7), Washington, DC. (LDA Consulting., 2012. Capital Bikeshare 2011 Member Survey Report. Washington, D.C.: LDA Consulting), Minnesota (Nice Ride Minnesota., 2010.* Nice Ride Minnesota Survey November 2010 *[Online]. Minnesota: Nice Ride Minnesota. Available: http://appv3.sgizmo.com/reportsview/?key=102593-416326-6d13ea0276ea0822c9f59f4411b6c779 [Accessed Accessed 20th June 2011]) and London (Transport for London., 2011. Barclays cycle hire customer satisfaction and usage: wave 2.* In: *Transport for London (ed.). London: Transport for London).*

Some evaluation studies have asked bike share members whether the availability of bike share has influenced their car ownership. *Capital Bikeshare* in Washington DC. as part of its regular member survey found that 44% of members didn't have access to a car, and another 20% of respondents said that they reduced their driving, by an average of 1565 miles per year, resulting in almost 10 million miles less driving (LDA Consulting, 2017). Members also reported using car services (e.g., Uber) less due to bike share (LDA Consulting, 2017). An earlier annual survey of *Capital Bikeshare* members found 5% of respondents reported selling a household vehicle since joining and 80% of these members said bike share was a factor in their decision to sell the vehicle (LDA Consulting, 2013). Notwithstanding the research undertaken by LDA Consulting for *Capital Bikeshare*, it is remarkable how little work has examined the impact of bike share on car ownership. A recent study looked into the impact of bike share on traffic congestion in U.S. cities with the findings suggesting a mix effect on congestion (Wang and Zhau, 2017). Using regression analysis, the researchers found that bike share was able to reduce peak hour congestion. For instance, the paper concluded that "a 1% increase in the population of cities without BSSs is associated with 0.6863% increase in congestion; however, a 1% growth in the population of cities with BSSs is associated with 0.0264% less increase in congestion" (Wang and Zhau, 2017, p. 151).

The results of this analysis demonstrate that in order for bike share programs to optimize their impact on reducing car use, it is necessary to implement measures focused on encouraging those currently making trips by car to use bike share. Results from a survey of non-bike share users from Brisbane (see Fishman et al., 2014b) suggest that this may be best achieved via policy changes that seek to increase the competitive advantage of bike share over the convenience of car use, and improving perceptions of rider safety, through the development of a network of protected bicycle lanes and paths.

5.2 Transport choice

Enhanced mobility options and convenience are two of the strongest, most consistent themes to emerge from research on why people use bike share (Fishman, 2015; Shaheen et al., 2013). Bike share has proven popular to combine with public transport, helping to make up for the inevitable deficiencies in the coverage or frequency of a city's public transport system (Fishman et al., 2014b). Another element of enhanced transport choice associated with bike share is improved transport flexibility. Unlike private cycling, bike share offers the user with the freedom to easily make one way cycling trips, and select another mode for a component of their day's travel, should it offer greater convenience.

Bike share has also been shown to increase the resilience and adaptability of the transport system. Findings suggest that when public transport fails (e.g., through a strike), bike share usage increases. For instance, Saberi et al. (2018) studied the impact of the London tube strike of 2015, via an analysis of over 1 million bike share trips. They found that during the period of the strike, the number of trips on London's bike share system increased and the average duration also increased dramatically, from 23 to 43 min. The researchers concluded that bike share can act to increase the resilience of transport networks, by providing a more flexible solution that can help to make up for the deficiency caused by public transport disruptions.

Bike share should not, however, be seen as mealy a competitor or replacement of public transport journeys. A consistent theme emerging from research is that bike share users regularly integrate their rides with public transport. For instance, an evaluation of dockless bike share usage in Seattle found that 75% of respondents had used bike share to access public transport and a third regularly access public transport with bike share (Seattle Department of Transportation, 2017).

One of the most important themes within this chapter is that people do not make transport mode decisions in isolation. The decision to use bike share will usually be as a result of weighing up the pros and cons of the different modes available. When bike share feels safe, is relatively fast and low cost, there is a heightened possibility it will be favored over other modes (Fishman, 2015). It is critical therefore that planners of bike share programs adopt a "thinking like a rider" mentality when designing a bike share system. This helps create a system that offers a more compelling value proposition to potential users. As the benefits of bike share are always dependent on the degree to which it is used, it must be designed to be competitive with other modes of transport, especially short car trips, if it is to maximize the benefits it offers (Wang and Zhau, 2017).

5.3 Health and safety

The rise in sedentary lifestyles is a major cause of disease and cycling has been shown to reduce the incident of diseases caused by a lack of physical activity (Götschi et al., 2016). Sedentary lifestyle disease is not the only population health issue bike share can influence. Air quality, transport safety and mental health are additional issues in which bike share has shown some impact in addressing. Several studies have attempted to quantify the health impacts of bike share, with some focused on one outcome variable, such as changes to physical activity levels, while others attempt to capture a larger range of outcomes. The most comprehensive examination of the health impacts of bike share was published in the British Medical Journal by Woodcock et al. (2014) and focused on the London bike share program. The researchers focused on three issues: physical activity, crashes and exposure to air pollution. This study used trip data to model the health impacts of the program via comparison to a scenario in which the program did not exist. Physical activity was found to increase considerably at the population level. The associated benefits were shown to differ by gender and age, with men's major benefit coming from reductions in ischemic heart disease, whereas women were more likely to benefit in terms of reductions in depression.

In the first multi-city analysis of the physical activity impacts of bike share, Fishman et al. (2015b) attempted to develop an estimate of the changes in physical activity levels due to bike share. Using data collected from the bike share systems in Melbourne, Brisbane, Washington, DC., London and Minneapolis/St. Paul, the researchers were interested in the net changes in physical activity by examining transfers from sedentary to active modes. The researchers used the mode substitution rates shown earlier in Fig. 9. Given that a kilometer walked consumes more energy than a kilometer cycled (Fishman et al., 2015a), the researchers needed to account for bike share trips that were previously walked, as this resulted in a net loss of physical activity.

The results from the Fishman et al. (2015b) study suggest an average of 60% of bike share trips replace sedentary modes, but when bike share replaces walking, a net reduction in physical activity results. Overall, however, bike share was found to have a positive impact on physical activity (see Fig. 10), leading to an additional 74 million minutes of physical activity in London through to 1.4 million minutes of physical activity in Minneapolis/St. Paul, for 2012.

Traffic injury has been a contentious issue for bike share, and it is often the case that an increase in crashes is predicted at the launch of a bike share program. A good example of this occurred in 2013, in the lead up to the launch of the Citi Bike program in New York City, in which a cycling expert predicted a doubling or a tripling of cycling fatalities (see Flegenheimer, 2013). Thankfully, these predictions have failed to materialize and there is now an

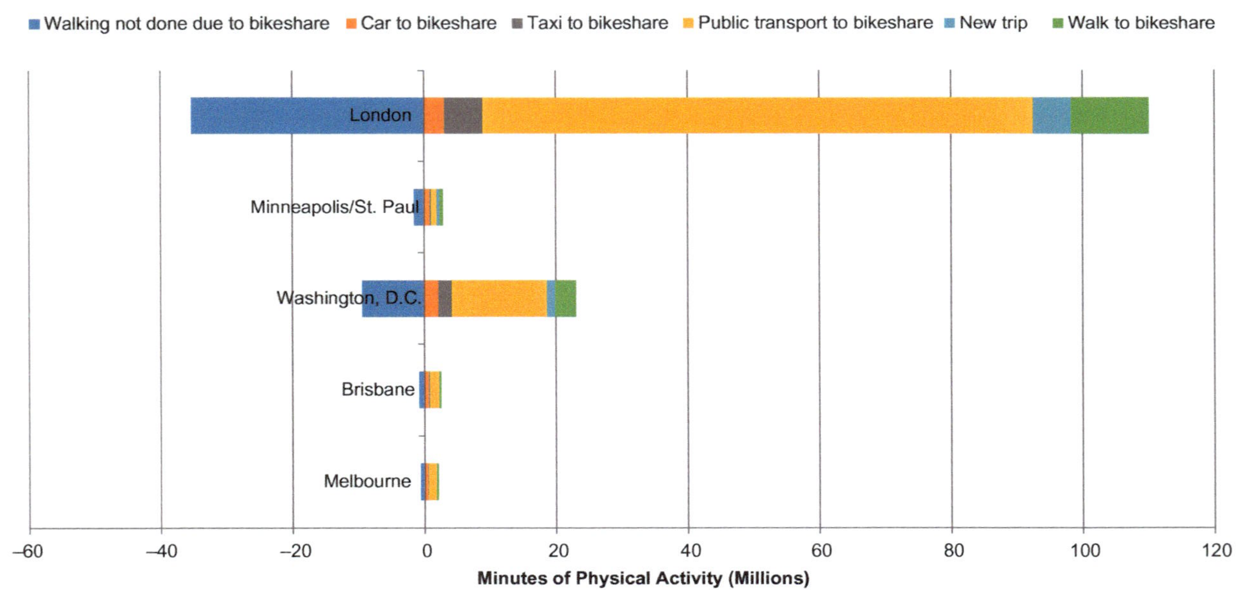

Fig. 10 Estimated changes to active travel due to bike share. *Source: Fishman, E., Washington, S., & Haworth, N. 2015c. Bikeshare's impact on active travel: Evidence from the United States, Great Britain, and Australia.* Journal of Transport & Health, *2*, *135-142.*

active sub-sector of the transport safety community examining why bike share appears to have a better safety record to cycling on private bikes.

Over a decade ago, Jacobsen (2003) published a landmark paper describing what has become known as "Safety in Numbers," showing that cyclists are less likely to be injured when volumes of cyclists are higher. As of December, 2017, only two fatalities have been recorded among those using U.S. bike share programs (Chicago and New York City). The fatality on Citi Bike occurred after 43 m trips had taken place since the system launched in May 2013. While the incidence of serious and fatal injuries appears to be lower than some initially expected, it is important to remember that may governments have adopted a Vision Zero approach to road safety, where the acceptable level of traffic fatality is zero. This means there is always more than can be done to reduce death and serious injury, and this includes the design of bike share programs and the street network they will use.

In 2014 a paper was published that sought to compare cities with, and cities without bike share programs, in terms of cycling injuries (Graves et al., 2014). The study attracted a great deal of attention due primarily to the fact that the researchers draw conclusions that seemed to partly ignore some of their most interesting findings (e.g., see Teschke and Winters, 2014; Woodcock and Goodman, 2014). Specifically, the researchers drew criticism for recommending more be done to provide helmets for bike share users despite their own data showing that head injuries from cycling went down in the cities with bike share programs. The data reported by Graves et al. (2014) are especially significant when considering that the overall amount of cycling increases after the introduction of a bike share program. This is consistent with the *Safety in Numbers* phenomenon (e.g., see Elvik, 2009), in which a rise in the amount of cycling does not lead to a proportional rise in the number of injuries. The analysis by Graves et al. (2014) occurred during a 24-month period before bike share implementation and also for a 12-month period post implementation. The non-bike share cities essentially acted as a control. The results are shown in Fig. 11.

In the first multi-country assessment of bike share safety that includes exposure factors, Fishman and Schepers (2016) assessed both the distance traveled and the number of reported injuries on bike share for 2013 in various U.S., European and Australian cities. The researchers compare the injury rates of the Paris and London bike share programs to the injury rates in the jurisdictions of which these are part. Bike share users were found to have a lower serious and slight injury rate than private cyclists in both London and Paris. This is consistent with the estimates for fatality rates and may show actual safety differences. Readers interested in examining

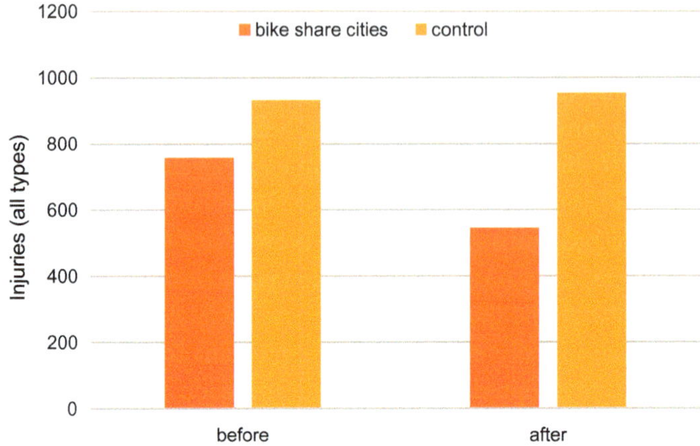

Fig. 11 Injuries (all types) bike share cities and non-bike share cities. *Source: Graves, J.M., Pless, B., Moore, L., Nathens, A.B., Hunte, G., Rivara, F.P. 2014. Public bicycle share programs and head injuries. Am. J. Public Health, 104, e106–e111.*

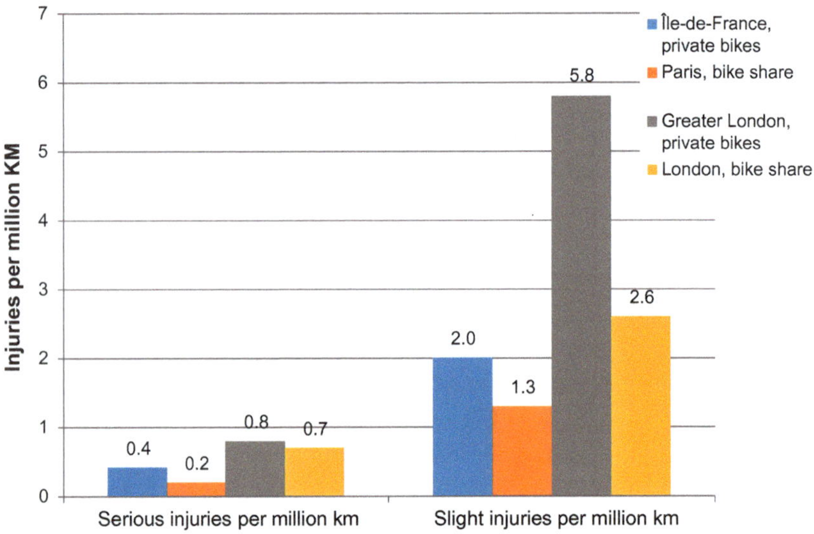

Fig. 12 Injuries per million KM traveled. *Source: Fishman, E., Schepers, P., 2016. Global bike share: what the data tells us about road safety. J. Safety Res. 56, 41–45.*

the methodology used to derive the data presented in Fig. 12 are encouraged to see the full paper, published in the Journal of Safety Research (see Fishman and Schepers, 2016).

The results presented in Fig. 12 suggest that bike share users are less likely than other cyclists to sustain fatal, severe or slight injuries. A relatively reliable measure for this is the fatality rate which was in the same range as the safest cycling countries in the world, the Netherlands and Denmark. According to the results of this analysis, a bike share user is half as likely to be fatally injured, per kilometer traveled, than a general cyclist, in jurisdictions in which a bike share program operates. However, the number of fatalities on which this comparison is based is still relatively low. Comparing serious and slight injuries leads to the same conclusion, but this comparison is hampered by the fact that the bike share data was based on information reported to operators while the numbers for other cyclists were based on police reported crashes. Although there are uncertainties, the fact that the literature and outcomes for all levels of injury severity point in the same direction yields some support for lower risk for bike share users compared to other cyclists.

One explanation for the higher levels of safety for bike share use might be that their speeds are substantially lower than for other cyclists. Bike share speeds are generally in the same range as the Netherlands. A slower speed increases the time available for cyclists to react to avoid crashes that may have occurred at higher velocities. It is also possible that motorists perceive bike share users to be less experienced and/or tourists and therefore display a greater level of caution, as revealed in qualitative research on perceptions of bike share (Fishman et al., 2012). The notion that drivers behave differently depending on the appearance of the cyclist has been established by Walker (2007) who found that drivers overtook closer to helmeted cyclists compared to those without a helmet. The upright position of bike share bikes may improve cyclists' visual observation of the road environment, potentially helping to avoid crashes. Finally, most bike share systems occupy the inner area of cities, which typically have better bicycle infrastructure than outer suburbs. Protected bike infrastructure is known to reduce crash risk between cyclists and motor vehicle drivers (Teschke et al., 2012).

In addition to the above benefits of bike share, it has also been found that bike share helps to normalize the image of cycling (Goodman et al., 2013). This is important in cities with very low bike mode share (less than ~4% of trips) because it is very often the case that cycling is seen by many to be a marginalized activity that is restricted to so-called MAMILS (middle aged men in lycra). Goodman et al. (2013) found that bike share riders in London were more likely to ride wearing regular clothes, with a gender balance closer to the population average. Bike share may therefore act to normalize cycling as an everyday transport option, rather than a sporting activity only available to a narrow segment of the population.

6. Mistakes in bike share: Lessons from history and how to avoid them

Bike share has generally been considered successful in the cities in which programs have been established, especially in the period prior to the introduction of dockless bike share. There are, however, instances in which bike share has failed to achieve the intented policy goals. Two examples can be found in Australia. Melbourne and Brisbane launched bike share programs in 2010, each of which have been characterized as having disappointing usage levels (e.g., see Atfield, 2016b, Fishman et al., 2015d, Fishman, 2012, Ward, 2011). Both systems typically have less than one trip per day per bike (Atfield, 2016a, Fishman, 2015, Atfield, 2016b). The intention of this section is to briefly identify the factors contributing to the low usage levels, in order to provide insights that may be useful for other cities considering establishing a bike share program, or seeking to improve the performance of the existing one.

6.1 Helmets

One factor that has been widely cited as a contributing factor to the low usage levels for the two Australian docked bike share programs are helmet laws. Australia is in a somewhat unique position as one of only a handful of countries with mandatory helmet laws, across all age groups and all riding contexts (Haworth et al., 2010). This makes bike share more difficult as it reduces the spontaneity with which people are able to use bike share (Fishman et al., 2014b). In some U.S. cities where helmet use is voluntary, bike share users are four times *less likely* to wear helmets than riders of private bicycles in the same city (Fischer et al., 2012). Research on Australian bike share users has found that they would use bike share more regularly if helmets use was voluntary rather than mandatory (Fishman et al., 2014a). A more detailed discussion on the issues associated with helmets in bike share schemes can be found in Fishman (2019).

6.2 System design

Since the 2010 launch of the Brisbane and Melbourne bike share programs, it has become recognized that the size of a system relative to the size of the city is an important determinant of scheme effectiveness (Institute for Transportation and Development Policy, 2018). Systems that are too small are not able to provide the coverage to enable the *network benefits* that help to boost the value proposition of bike share, relative to other transport modes. It is, however, important to recognize that the size of a system is not the only determining factor of system success, and Médard de Chardon et al. (2017), in their analysis of 75 different systems actually found system size to be less important than many other researchers have previously stated. Médard de Chardon et al. argued that system expansion should not be the only factor governing overall system performance. Nevertheless, without a sufficient set of origins and destination options that a large system provides, the ability of bike share to meet a population's travel needs will be limited. The former Chicago Transportation Commissioner Gabe Klein, explaining bike share, said "I knew that any sort of nodal business was only as effective as the number of nodes you have" (Vanderbilt, 2013). The New York City Department of Transportation, in a lengthy investigation of the applicability of bike share for that city reached a similar conclusion to Klein, noting "Evidence from bike-share programs around the world suggests that small programs do not provide meaningful transportation, health or economic development gains nor do they provide a significant basis from which the city could evaluate the effectiveness of the program" (New York City Department Of City Planning, 2009, p. 100).

6.3 Bicycle infrastructure

As described in Fig. 2, one of the critical elements of the transport system is "*rights of way*" and for bike share, this means a coherent network of quality bicycle lanes and paths. The bicycle infrastructure network is far from complete in Melbourne (more than 60% of the Principal Bicycle Network is "proposed") and is even less mature in Brisbane. Safety issues remain one of the most significant deterrents to cycling in Melbourne (Pucher et al., 2010) and Brisbane (Fishman et al., 2012). In many cities that have established well used bike share programs (e.g., Barcelona, New York City, Paris), the dedicated program of bicycle network expansion occurred in the years leading up to launching a bike share program. Melbourne and Brisbane launched bike share without a sufficient network of protected bicycle infrastructure to support strong usage levels. This serves as a valuable lesson for other cities without a comprehensive network of bicycle friendly infrastructure that are either considering a bike share program or looking to enhance an existing one. While it is never easy to convert city streets to become more cycle friendly, it is an important prerequisite to a successful bike share program.

6.4 Sign up process

The sign up process required before one is able to begin riding a bike share bike has improved significantly in recent years, primarily through the widespread use of mobile devices as the primary interface. Docked systems, especially those developed prior to the widespread adoption of the smartphone, such as Brisbane's *CityCycle* scheme, required a more lengthy procedure. In Brisbane's case, this was taken to an extreme, where users were unable to sign up on the spot via a credit card swipe at a payment kiosk. For more than a year after the launch of *CityCycle*, prospective users were required to call a number, during office hours, to manually sign up to the program. Initially, these callers were required to listen to up to 24 min of legal disclaimer notices before being granted access to the bicycles. Users could of course sign up online, but would have to wait between 5 and 10 days before receiving their membership material. With most bike share trips being under 16 min, it appears members of the public viewed these delays as unreasonable and chose to make alternative travel arrangements. Finally, for the first 2 years, members were locked out of the system between 10 pm and 5 am, and this, in addition to the aforementioned issues were key frustrations for members (Fishman et al., 2012, Roy Morgan Research, 2013) that ultimately impacted on their wiliness to renew membership. This was a lost opportunity that failed to capitalize on the interest people had in trying Brisbane's bike share program. While the sign up process has been somewhat streamlined, and the user fees substantially reduced, the reputation damage this had on *CityCycle's* "brand" may have had a lasting impact on ridership. The lesson for other cities interested in maximizing bike share ridership is to create a system in which the time taken from initial interest, to riding, is minimized.

6.5 Lack of consultation

One distinctive factor in the development of the Melbourne and Brisbane bike share programs was the lack of consultation and planning. Unlike most North American bike share programs, there were no community outreach or stakeholder engagement sessions with the transport community regarding the possible design features to maximize the success of the bike share program. No consultation was offered to refine the type of bicycles offered, the placement of the docking stations, sign up procedure or helmets. The following section elaborates on each of these issues, in an effort to assist other cities seeking to establish a bike share program.

6.6 Launch season

The Melbourne bike share program launched at the beginning of winter, and even in Australia, this led to a lower level of use at the crucial first few months of the program. Cycling levels drop in winter (Ahmed et al., 2010). A winter launch can have a strong and persistent reduction in usage levels. Research from Australia has shown that one of the most important influences on people's interest in bike share is whether they see other people using it (Fishman, 2019; Fishman and Davies, 2016; Fishman et al., 2012). For the Melbourne bike share program, people became accustomised to seeing the bikes sit unused and this created the reinforcing negative feedback loop that compounded the problem of starting in winter. The lesson from this experience is that bike share programs should begin during the season most conductive to riding. The more people see others rider the bikes, as close as possible after launch, the more likely the system will be viewed positively by others.

6.7 Equity in bike share

Despite the ability for cities and its inhabitants to have improved mobility options as a result of bike share, questions about who is able to access the system are still apparent for many. By looking at demographic data for bike share schemes, it is apparent that many of the users are wealthy, highly educated, white males (Fishman, 2015; Ricci, 2015; Shaheen et al., 2012b). To an extent, this may be due to the preference of such demographic groups to use bike share, for environmental, health, or social reasons. Looking at it another way, the demographics of bike share use is driven by the spatial locating of bike share in the wealthier areas of cities. In reviewing the spatial locations of different bike share schemes in the United States, Smith et al. (2015) found that 35 of the schemes had placed over 53% of docking stations within the top quintile of economically advantaged Census blocks. Likewise for Canadian cities with docked bike share schemes, Hosford and Winters (2018) found that socio-economically advantaged areas had better access to docking stations than disadvantaged areas.

With the introduction of dockless schemes, the ability to provide a more agile bike share scheme has become possible. The ability of dockless systems to be ridden freely throughout the city and locked at the destination without the need for a docking station or specialist infrastructure offers the potential for a more equitable bike share system. To date, limited research on the spatial equity of dockless bike share schemes has been done. One recent study

(Mooney et al., 2019) analyzed the trial of dockless bike share in Seattle and found promising spatial equity characteristics, though more highly educated areas were serviced with slightly more dockless bikes.

In addition to spatial equity, efforts have been undertaken with many bike share schemes to improve access for everyone. In particular, the *Better Bike Share Partnership* in the United States was set up in 2014 to directly address barriers to access for low-income groups and communities of color. Programs funded through the *Better Bike Share Partnership* include providing reduced fare rates, developing cash payment options, locating new docking stations in underserved neighborhoods, as well as outreach programs for low income areas. As more bike share schemes move away from publicly funded institutions to privately operated schemes, it is important that equitable access to bike share is continually sought, whether through regulation, grants programs, or through open dialogue between operators and the communities they operate in.

7. The coming revolution in e-bike share

The sharp growth in bike share has coincided with a similarly rapid growth in e-bike performance, affordability and usage. In recent years a number of cities have launched bike sharing programs that offer electric assistance bikes, known as pedelecs (e-bikeshare). Enabling the rider to maintain speed with less effort, especially in topographically challenging cities, has resulted in a strong consumer preference for e-bikeshare. Birmingham, Alabama, launched a system that uses a combination of conventional and electric assist bikesharing bikes. The electric assist bikes are ridden three to four times as much as the conventional bicycles (Bewegen Technologies Inc, 2016).

Perhaps the most prominent example of combing e-bikes and bike share came when Uber purchased JUMP, the dockless bike share provider. In San Francisco, the JUMP bikes were made available through the Uber App, and usage data shows a strong shift toward the e-bikes, and a reduction in trip numbers in Uber motor vehicles (McFarland, 2018). The strongest shift toward the e-bikes occurred during commuting and working hours on weekdays, suggesting the trips were transport rather than recreation based. The largest spikes in JUMP usage came at the height of the morning and afternoon peak hour (McFarland, 2018). The founder of JUMP, Ryan Rzepecki has said that the electric assist element of a bike share bike, when produced at scale, is only around $US200-$300 extra per bike (Marshall, 2018) and therefore, given the extra utility it offers, will become the obvious choice for bike share provision in the future.

8. Charting a new course in bike share literature

There is a growing need to chart a new course in shared mobility research. With the exponential growth in bike share from docked to dockless systems, as well as the introduction of e-bike share, new research questions have emerged that must be addressed. This is amplified by new shared mobility platforms including e-scooters and rideables. Many of the research papers reviewed in this chapter, and many of the recent and forthcoming papers on dockless bike share continue along the same research paradigm set out from docked bike share. While there will continue to be elements that overlap between docked and dockless systems, the latter presents new challenges that will require new approaches to research. This section explores several existing research gaps and state the case for a new direction in shared mobility research.

8.1 Differences in business models

This shift toward fully commercial bike share programs raise questions regarding the economic sustainability of the business model. The industry has been in a state of flux and many companies have ceased operations less than a year from entering some markets. Moreover, even established, large scale dockless bike share operators are failing to make a profit, and this raises questions about their long-term financial viability. This is important because it disrupts a city's ability to provide long-term transport options for citizens, in addition to wasting the material resources involved in the manufactor of these bicycle fleets. If for-profit bike share schemes are to contribute to the long-term transport operation, further research is required to determine its ability to provide a level of service commensurate with the expectations of the public. All too often dockless bikes are found in a state of mechanical disrepair that make riding unpleasant or even dangerous. Research that helps to find a middle ground that is affordable to government, but offers sufficient subsidy to allow the private sector to provide a level of service that offers the user with a well-balanced, well-maintained bike share system is crucial.

In order to bridge the research gap between docked and dockless bike share, it will also be important for dockless bike share operators to provide the data on ridership their GPS based systems generate. In most cases, this will require the government authority in which the bike share operations to mandate an Open Data policy, allowing researchers to examine anonymous riding data.

8.2 *E*-scooters, rideables, and innovative mobility

In the last few years, there has been an explosion in product offers for new personal mobility devices. These devices have sought to improve mobility options for short trips through new technology. These include "hoverboards," Onewheels, electric skateboards and scooters. Beginning in the United States with companies such as *Bird* and *Lime*, electric scooter share has expanded rapidly across the globe. Operating under similar business models as dockless bike share, this new mobility option offers fresh insights into how people choose to move around a city. Initial reports have also highlighted increased safety concerns regarding the use of electric scooters compared to other modes of transport. Further research will be required to fully understand the safety implications for new mobility devices, including electric scooters. Concerns about the lifecycle of new mobility devices has also been raised. Images of dockless bike share "graveyards" in China and internationally threaten the long-term sustainability of dockless schemes and the environmental impacts. Persistent theft and vandalism of dockless bikes and e-scooters also calls into question the ability for operators to maintain an economically viable business model.

8.3 Shared mobility and community backlash

As part of the growth in shared mobility, and in particular the shift toward dockless and free-floating shared mobility, we have seen a rise in theft, vandalism, and public criticism of these new systems. Images of dockless bikes hanging from trees and retrieved from the bottom of rivers, to videos of people setting fire to e-scooters, have become common sights within cities. The extent of community backlash has caused many operators to cease business in some cities or even go out of business as a result. The causes for such public action against dockless operators varies, from poor quality bikes and operation methods, an "act now, ask for forgiveness later" business attitude, and a lack of rights to space within the city as discussed earlier in this chapter. If we are to expect shared mobility and MaaS to take on more of the transport task in the future, it is imperative to better understand the relationship the community has with these services.

9. Conclusion

This review has provided a synthesis of some of the research focused on the growing topic of bike share. The expansion of topics within the bike share literature has meant that it has not been possible to explore all the issues the research covers. Bike share has expanded rapidly over recent years, and dockless bike share, owning to the ease with which they can be produced and deployed has accounted for much of the recent growth. Bike share, it has been shown, can have an important positive impact on the key challenges many urban regions are currently facing. Bike share has been shown to have a positive impact on congestion, emissions and physical activity. Bike share has not, however, been universally successful. This chapter has provided examples of cities that have introduced under used bike share programs, caused by a variety of factors including insufficient infrastructure, helmet laws, poor customer experience and a failure to engage with the community during the planning process.

Electric assist and other technologies are likely to continue to transform the bike share industry, helping to boost the value proposition it offers. While the tech industry has helped to make the vehicle and the bike share system easier to use, in many cities, the challenge of allocating the space and infrastructure to support safe cycling continues to be one of the main barriers that will need to be overcome should bike share (and cycling generally) achieve its potential to make cities more productive, sustainable and liveable.

References

Ahmed, F., Rose, G., Jacob, C., 2010. Impact of weather on commuter cyclist behaviour and implications for climate change adaptation. In: Australasian Transport Research Forum. Canberra.

Atfield, C., 2016a. Brisbane Deputy Mayor Adrian Schrinner Backs Voluntary Helmet Trial for Cyclists. Sydney Morning Herald.

Atfield, C., 2016b. Mayor Defends Cost of Brisbane's CityCycle Scheme. Brisbane Times.

Bewegen Technologies Inc, 2016. 16th December, RE: discussion between Marc Delesclefs (Bewegen) and Elliot Fishman (Institute for Sensible Transport). (Type to Fishman, E).

Buehler, R., Pucher, J., 2020. The Future of City Cycling. MIT Press, Cambridge, MA.

DeMaio, P., 2009. Bike-sharing: history, impacts, models of provision, & future. J. Public Transport. 12, 41–56.

Elvik, R., 2009. The non-linearity of risk and the promotion of environmentally sustainable transport. Accid. Anal. Prev. 41, 849–855.

Fischer, C.M., Sanchez, C.E., Pittman, M., Milzman, D., Volz, K.A., Huang, H., Gautam, S., Sanchez, L.D., 2012. Prevalence of bicycle helmet use by users of public Bikeshare programs. Ann. Emerg. Med. 60, 228–231.

Fishman, E., 2012. Fixing Australian bike share goes beyond helmet laws [Online]. The Conversation. Available, https://theconversation.edu.au/fixing-australian-bike-share-goes-beyond-helmet-laws-10229. (Accessed Accessed 26th June 2013).

Fishman, E., 2015. Bikeshare: a review of recent literature. Transp. Rev. 36, 1–22.

Fishman, E., 2017. Bike Share Parking Infrastructure Guidelines. Prepared by the Institute for Sensible Transport for VicRoad, Melbourne.

Fishman, E., 2019. Bike Share. Routledge (forthcoming).

Fishman, E., Davies, L., 2016. Bike Share at Western Sydney University Parramatta. Institute for Sensible Transport, Melbourne.

Fishman, E., Schepers, P., 2016. Global bike share: what the data tells us about road safety. J. Safety Res. 56, 41–45.

Fishman, E., Washington, S., Haworth, N., 2012. Barriers and facilitators to public bicycle scheme use: a qualitative approach. Transport. Res. F: Traffic Psychol. Behav. 15, 686–698.

Fishman, E., Washington, S., Haworth, N., 2014a. Bike Share's impact on car use: evidence from the United States, Great Britain, and Australia. Transp. Res. Part D: Transp. Environ. 31, 7.

Fishman, E., Washington, S., Haworth, N., Mazzei, A., 2014b. Barriers to bikesharing: an analysis from Melbourne and Brisbane. J. Transp. Geogr. 41, 325–337.

Fishman, E., BÖcker, L., Helbich, M., 2015a. Adult active transport in the Netherlands: an analysis of its contribution to physical activity requirements. PLoS ONE 10, e0121871.

Fishman, E., Washington, S., Haworth, N., 2015b. Bikeshare's impact on active travel: evidence from the United States, Great Britain, and Australia. J. Transp. Health 2, 135–142.

Fishman, E., Washington, S., Haworth, N., Watson, A., 2015d. Factors influencing bike share membership: an analysis of Melbourne and Brisbane. Transp. Res. A 71, 17–30.

Flegenheimer, M., 2013. No Riders Killed in First 5 Months of New York City Bike-Share Program [Online]. New York Times, New York. Available, http://www.nytimes.com/2013/11/05/nyregion/no-riders-killed-in-first-5-months-of-new-york-city-bike-share-program.html?_r=0. (Accessed 23rd December 2014).

Fuller, G., Waitt, G., Buchanan, I., 2018. The Problem isn't Dockless Share Bikes. It's the Lack of Bike Parking. The Conversation.

Giles-Corti, B., Vernez-Moudon, A., Reis, R., Turrell, G., Dannenberg, A.L., Badland, H., Foster, S., Lowe, M., Sallis, J.F., Stevenson, M., Owen, N., 2016. City planning and population health: a global challenge. Lancet. 388, 2912–2924.

Goodman, A., Green, J., Woodcock, J., 2013. The role of bicycle sharing systems in normalising the image of cycling: an observational study of London cyclists. J. Transp. Health 1, 5–8.

Goodwin, P., Van Dender, K., 2013. 'Peak Car' — themes and issues. Transp. Rev. 33, 243–254.

Götschi, T., Garrard, J., Giles-Corti, B., 2016. Cycling as a part of daily life: a review of health perspectives. Transp. Rev. 36 (1), 45–71. https://doi.org/10.1080/01441647.2015.1057877.

Graves, J.M., Pless, B., Moore, L., Nathens, A.B., Hunte, G., Rivara, F.P., 2014. Public bicycle share programs and head injuries. Am. J. Public Health 104, e106–e111.

Haworth, N., Schramm, A., King, M., Steinhardt, D., 2010. Bicycle Helmet Research. Centre for Accident Research and Road Safety, Queensland.

Hoffmann, C., Kandt, J., Smith, D., Graff, A., 2015. In: Griffiths, P. (Ed.), Toward New Urban Mobility: The case of London and Berlin. London School of Economics & the Innovation Centre for Mobility and Societal Change (InnoZ) GmbH, London.

Hosford, K., Winters, M., 2018. Who are public bicycle share programs serving? An evaluation of the equity of spatial access to bicycle share service areas in Canadian cities. Transp. Res. Rec. 2672, 42–50.

Hure, M., Passalacqua, A., 2017. La Rochelle, France, and the invention of bike sharing public policy in the 1970. J. Transp. Hist. 38, 106–123.
Institute for Transportation & Development Policy, 2018. The Bikeshare Planning Guide. Institute for Transportation & Development Policy, New York City.
Jacobsen, P.L., 2003. Safety in numbers: more walkers and bicyclists, safer walking and bicycling. Inj. Prev. 9, 205–209.
Kager, R., Bertolini, L., Brömmelstroet, M., 2016. Characterisation of and reflections on the synergy of bicycles and public transport. Transp. Res. A Policy Pract. 85, 208–219.
Kaufman, S.M., Gordon-Koven, L., Levenson, N., Moss, M.L., 2015. Citi Bike: The First Two Years. Rudin Center for transportation policy and management, New York City.
Lansell, K., 2011. Melbourne Bike Share and Public Transport Integration. Master of Urban Planning Minor thesis, University of Melbourne.
LDA Consulting, 2013. 2013 Capital Bikeshare Member Survey Report. Washington, D.C.: Capital Bikeshare.
LDA Consulting, 2017. 2016 Capital Bikeshare Member Survey Report. LDA Consulting, Washington, D.C.
Llich, I., 1973. Energy and Equity. Harper & Row.
Marshall, A., 2018. Electric Bikes Want to Take on Everyone—Even. Uber.
Martens, K., 2004. The bicycle as a feedering mode: experiences from three European countries. Transportation Research Part D: Transport and Environment 9, 281–294.
McFarland, M., 2018. Uber's e-Bikes Are Cannibalizing Rides from Uber's Cars. CNN Business.
Médard de Chardon, C., Caruso, G., Thomas, I., 2017. Bicycle sharing system 'success' determinants. Transp. Res. A Policy Pract. 100, 202–214.
Meddin, R., 2018. The Bike-sharing World Map [Online]. The Bike-sharing Blog, Available, www.bikesharingmap.com. (Accessed).
Meddin, R., DeMaio, P., 2016. The Bike-sharing World the Last Week of December 2015 [Online]. The Bike-sharing Blog, Available, http://bike-sharing.blogspot.com.au/2015/12/the-bike-sharing-world-last-week-of.html. (Accessed).
Ministerie Van Verkeer En Waterstaat, 2009. Cycling in the Netherlands. Ministerie van Verkeer en Waterstaat.
Mooney, S.J., Hosford, K., Howe, B., Yan, A., Winters, M., Bassok, A., 2019. Freedom from the station: spatial equity in access to dockless bike share. J. Transp. Geogr. 74, 91–96.
NACTO, 2018. *Bike Share in the U.S. 2017* [Online]. National Association of City Transportation Officials. Available, https://nacto.org/bike-share-statistics-2017/, (Accessed).
New York City Department Of City Planning, 2009. Bike-Share: Opportunities in New York City. City of New York, New York.
Parkes, S.D., Marsden, G., Shaheen, S.A., Cohen, A.P., 2013. Understanding the diffusion of public bikesharing systems: evidence from Europe and North America. J. Transp. Geogr. 31, 94–103.
Pucher, J., Greaves, S., Garrard, J., 2010. Cycling down under: a comparative analysis of bicycling trends and policies in Sydney and Melbourne. J. Transp. Geogr. 19, 332–345.
Ricci, M., 2015. Bike sharing: a review of evidence on impacts and processes of implementation and operation. Res. Transp. Bus. Manag. 15, 28–38.
Roy Morgan Research, 2013. Brisbane City Council CityCycle Customer Satisfaction Research. Commissioned by Brisbane City Council, Brisbane.
Saberi, M., Ghamami, M., Gu, Y., Shojaei, M.H., FISHMAN, E., 2018. Understanding the impacts of a public transit disruption on bicycle sharing mobility patterns: a case of tube strike in London. J. Transp. Geogr. 66, 154–166.

Sallis, J.F., Bull, F., Burdett, R., Frank, L.D., Griffiths, P., Giles-Corti, B., Stevenson, M., 2016. Use of science to guide city planning policy and practice: how to achieve healthy and sustainable future cities. Lancet. 388, 2936–2947.
Schimmelpennink, L., 2014. In: Fishman, E. (Ed.), Dutch Transport Innovation. Institute for Sensible Transport, Amsterdam.
Seattle Department of Transportation, 2017. 2017 Free-Floating Bike Share Pilot Evaluation Report. Seattle Department of Transportation, Seattle.
Shaheen, S., Cohen, A., 2018. Shared ride services in North America: definitions, impacts, and the future of pooling. Transp. Rev. 39 (4), 427–442.
Shaheen, S., Guzman, S., Zhang, H., 2010. Bikesharing in Europe, the Americas, and Asia. Transp. Res. Rec. J. Transp. Res. Board 2143, 159–167.
Shaheen, S., Guzman, S., Zhang, H., 2012a. Chapter 9: Bikesharing across the Globe. In: City Cycling. MIT press, Boston.
Shaheen, S., Martin, E., Cohen, A.P., Finson, R., 2012b. Public Bikesharing in North America: Early Operator and User Understanding. Mineta Transportation Institute, San Jose.
Shaheen, S., Cohen, A.P., Martin, E.W., 2013. Public Bikesharing in North America: early operator understanding and emerging trends. Transp. Res. Rec. J. Transp. Res. Board 2387, 83–92.
Smith, C., Oh, J.S., Lei, C., 2015. Exploring the Equity Dimensions of US Bicycle Sharing Systems. Tennessee State University, Tennessee.
Stapleton, L., Sorrell, S., Schwanen, T., 2017. Peak car and increasing rebound: a closer look at car travel trends in Great Britain. Transp. Res. Part D: Transp. Environ. 53, 217–233.
Stevenson, M., Thompson, J., de Sá, T.H., Ewing, R., Mohan, D., McClure, R., Roberts, I., Tiwari, G., Giles-Corti, B., Sun, X., Wallace, M., Woodcock, J., 2016. Land use, transport, and population health: estimating the health benefits of compact cities. Lancet 388, 2925–2935.
Teschke, K., Winters, M., 2014. Letter to editor. Am. J. Public Health. http://cyclingincities-spph.sites.olt.ubc.ca/files/2014/06/Graves-AJPH-as-submitted.pdf.
Teschke, K., Harris, M.A., Reynolds, C.C.O., Winters, M., Babul, S., Chipman, M., Cusimano, M.D., Brubacher, J.R., Hunte, G., Friedman, S.M., Monro, M., Shen, H., Vernich, L., Cripton, P.A., 2012. Route infrastructure and the risk of injuries to bicyclists: a case-crossover study. Am. J. Public Health 102, 2336–2343.
Transport For London, 2018. Santander Cycles Customer Satisfaction and Usage Survey Casual Users Only: Quarter 2 2017/18. Transport for London, London.
Van Dender, K., Clever, M., 2013. Recent Trends in Car Usage in Advanced Economies: Slower Growth Ahead?; Summary and Conclusions. Organisation for Economic Development and Cooperation, Paros.
Vanderbilt, T., 2013. The Best Bike-Sharing Program in the United States. Washington Post, Slate.com.
Walker, I., 2007. Drivers overtaking bicyclists: objective data on the effects of riding position, helmet use, vehicle type and apparent gender. Accid. Anal. Prev. 39, 417–425.
Wang, M., Zhau, X., 2017. Bike-sharing systems and congestion: evidence from US cities. J. Transp. Geogr. 65, 147–154.
Ward, C., 2011. Two in Three CityCycle Bikes Sitting Idle. Brisbane Times.
Woodcock, J., Goodman, A., 2014. Hard Evidence: Do Bikeshare Schemes Lead to More Head Injuries Among Cyclists? The Conversation, Available, http://theconversation.com/hard-evidence-do-bikeshare-schemes-lead-to-more-head-injuries-among-cyclists-30135. (Accessed 28th August).
Woodcock, J., Tainio, M., Cheshire, J., O'brien, O., Goodman, A., 2014. Health effects of the London bicycle sharing system: health impact modelling study. BMJ 348, g425.
Yanocha, D., 2018. Optimizing Dockless Bikeshare and Other Private New Mobility Services. Prepared for the OECD, New York City.

CHAPTER SEVEN

Conclusion

Elliot Fishman*
Director of the Institute for Sensible Transport, Melbourne, VIC, Australia
*Corresponding author: e-mail address: info@sensibletransport.org.au

Abstract

This book has captured an up to date review of the literature regarding many of the disruptive transport technologies that are currently being introduced or are set to have an impact on our cities in the near future. Driverless cars, e-bike share and large scale app based travel aggregators are likely to transform the ownership model that has dominated transport for more than a century. While it is clear an 'access over ownership' model will play a much larger role within the transport sector, the degree to which this provides maximum benefit is highly contingent on effective government regulation. It is inevitable that road user pricing will need to be introduced in order to better manage future demand for road access in the future.

Keywords: Mobility as a service, Driverless vehicle, Bike share, Road user pricing, Disruptive transport

As the proportion of the world's population living in cities continues to grow, toward an estimated 70% by 2050, the way we use space and resources will need to be critically examined. There are few examples of a poorer use of space and resources than the manner in which we plan transport systems in our cities. Up to 50% of the land area of some cities is dedicated to motor vehicles (either as roads or parking), yet most of our city trips are short (under 5 km) and our vehicle occupancy is little more than one person per vehicle, and this occupancy is at its lowest during peak hour. Transport is one of the fastest growing sources of greenhouse gas emissions, and congestion limits the productivity and potential for human interaction that have attracted people to cities for thousands of years. To say there is room for improvement when discussing the urban transport challenge is a dramatic understatement.

The sharing economy, facilitated by the ubiquity of the Internet and the smartphone, has begun to disrupt the ownership model of transport that has dominated the transport sector for well over 50 years. Young people do not see the acquisition of a drivers license as a rite of passage in the same way they did a generation ago, and per capita car ownership has begun to reduce.

ISSN 2543-0009
https://doi.org/10.1016/bs.atpp.2019.10.003

Even the former CEO of the Ford Motor Company, Mark Fields appears to understand the trend; *'We look at changing consumer buying behaviors, particularly millennials in urban areas. They want access versus ownership.'*

Yet despite these positive signs, the overall number of vehicles has never been higher, and in some cities with a strong Uber/Lyft/ride sourcing presence, congestion has been made *worse* rather than better. This highlights a central, unifying theme within this Volume. If left entirely to the market, without policy and regulatory involvement by government, many of the developments in transport technology could, perversely, *exacerbate* our transport challenges. In particular, the prospect of fleets of driverless cars, cannibalizing public transport patronage, walking and cycling, by offering door to door convenience at a price comparable to public transport, threatens to erode any of the advancements in sustainable transport promised by the MaaS future.

For the sharing economy to make the gains in transport sustainability that cities so desperately need, it is inevitable that government will need to change the way people pay for road use. Those that drive more will need to pay more and those driving less will pay less. Doing away with fixed fees (such as registration/insurance) and moving toward variable charging is something that transport economists have long argued. The introduction of electric, autonomous vehicles makes this change in pricing policy for road use all but inevitable, it helps to replace the revenue from fuel excise that will diminish as more of the fleet becomes electric. This will change how people pay for car use in line with the way people typically pay for public transport (i.e., if you travel more, you pay more). Importantly, moving toward a network based, road user fee will provide the pricing signals to moderate people's appetite for car-based mobility and help to ensure that walking, cycling and public transport still appeals in a world of driverless, electric mobility.

Of all the different forms of shared mobility currently available, bike share has shown tremendous grow, in overall units, and usage. This includes being used as a first mile/last mile solution to support public transport. The bike share industry is currently in a state of flux after a dramatic increase in the global fleet caused by the rise of dockless, fully commercial (though rarely profit making) systems that have been introduced to cities around the world in the 2014–18 period. What the future holds for bike share is not entirely clear, though a shift toward higher quality, electric-assist bikes that have greater coordination with wider government transport policy appears to be emerging following the period of poor quality, uncoordinated dockless systems.

This volume has identified that the prospect of reducing the need to own a vehicle is the key potential benefit arising from the current period of technological development, such as the driverless car. By creating an *access over ownership* model, the potential exists for people to have the incentive to make more efficient choices regarding their mode of travel. Rather than the car being the default mode of transport, as it has become for many, people have the incentive to choose the most appropriate mode to meet their purpose. In some cases this may be a car, sometimes as the only occupant, at other times shared. In other circumstances it may be public transport, walking or cycling (or a combination of modes). As the world continues to become more urbanized, the emergence of shared transport options holds the prospect of arresting and reversing the dominance of the car ownership model that has prevailed since the Second World War. While technology companies have exercised their agility and appetite for innovation, it is now up to government to be equally agile in adapting the regulatory environment they control, to ensure cities and communities get the very most out of what this paradigm promises.

FSC
www.fsc.org
MIX
Papier | Fördert gute Waldnutzung
FSC® C083411

Kolibri 360 GmbH
Ferdinand-Jühlke-Straße 7
99095 Erfurt, Deutschland
produktsicherheit@kolibri360.de